THE FINANCIAL
ADVISOR
TO BUILDING
WEALTH

™

*PURSUING PROSPERITY
WITH FINANCIAL EDUCATION*

Thomas Herold – Summer 2011 Edition

The Financial Advisor to Building Wealth

Pursuing Prosperity
with Financial Education

Summer 2011 Edition

Revision 1.1

Thomas Herold
Dream Manifesto, LLC.

www.wealthbuildingcourse.com

Table of Contents

INTRODUCTION

"Pursuing Prosperity with Financial Education"

Welcome to the Financial Advisor to Building Your Wealth

It's my pleasure to present the summer 2011 edition of our quarterly publication 'Financial Advisor to Building Wealth'.

Just take a moment and think about what wealth means to you. If you're like most folk, you think it's all about money. It was for me too, until I decided to explore the topic more deeply and really consider what makes us wealthy, prosperous people. Wealth, for me, is not merely material possessions: it's your health, your lifestyle and relationships, even your mental abilities.

Curious yet? If you still think money has anything to do with wealth, you'll be in for a big surprise when you read this issue. My main aim, and the inspiration for my website and the whole of my work, is to help you learn about finance like I did – to help you transform your life, leave the past behind and take control of your wealth. Now, you might think financial terminology is about as interesting as a bag of rice falling off a shelf in China. But these days, one of the most essential and precious gifts you can give yourself is a financial education - especially given the worldwide economic crisis we are all experiencing.

Humanity is embarking on the biggest transfer of wealth in history. You may have sensed it already, and you're right: wealth is flowing at breathtaking speeds away from the financially uneducated towards people who know about finance and, crucially, how to use that knowledge to their advantage.

The current international financial crisis is a direct outcome of government and bank interventions. It's time for us to open our eyes to this and start to protect ourselves.

You might have heard the phrase, "If you always do what you've always done, you'll always get what you've always got." There's no question that, in order to secure your future and live a life that you're in control of, you must take on the task of understanding what is happening to your hard-earned money.

Once you grasp and unravel the hidden agenda of a few powerful people, you will be able to choose and reclaim your financial freedom. At the moment, this may all sound like a conspiracy theory to you; however, the research and facts contained in this book will provide you with enough evidence that there is a plan behind all this, which right now is serving other people, not you.

You'll realize that this plan is nothing new, and that the past shows similar attempts at monetary control and failure. Learning about these will make you better able to react to the present, and start creating wealth for yourself, rather than other people.

I've structured the articles into several categories. Feel free to skip between them and simply read what interests you most. Remember: this is not a course that you're doing for anyone else. This is a gift to yourself. Read the articles that apply to you, and in doing so you will broaden your knowledge and feel more qualified to keep learning and growing your wealth.

All the articles have been taken from the Wealth Building Course website and assembled here for you to make your financial learning simpler and more convenient. I've left out several articles which focused on issues that have now been overtaken by events. The situation is constantly changing, but the articles here have been carefully selected for their continuing relevance.

Enjoy your reading and always keep learning. Allow your mind to open up to new ideas. Believe that you can change your approach to wealth, and transform your life. As Steve Jobs once said: "Stay hungry, stay foolish."

Thomas Herold

Introduction

<u>INVESTING</u>

"Putting Energy to Work"

Investing

How the Weak Supply Will Drive Up the Price of Silver

Over the past decade, the supply of newly refined silver has been less than that required to satisfy demand, with this deficit being largely addressed by reducing actual stocks of silver that had been built up during the 1980s, when silver supplies exceeded demand.

The market for the metal has been in a supply deficit since around 1990 although you would never know it due to artificial controls on price through so-called silver "leasing."

As a result of a 60-year structural deficit, we have exhausted just about all the world's existing silver inventory. That includes just those inventories that have been rigorously stockpiled by various governments around the world. We're way overdue for a run on silver. When the unavoidable silver run occurs, there will be no one to douse the price fire. This cannot be said about any other commodity at present, even gold.

The less supply there is of something to invest in, the greater the price impact will be when demand appears. Demand creates price, up or down. Silver is going up.

No More Silver for the Mint

Silver is no longer used in the minting of dimes, nickels, and quarters. This has been the case since 1965. The U.S.

Mint now uses zinc, in an alloy of 75% copper and 25% nickel, in place of silver for nickels and dimes. Quarters and halves contain a slightly different zinc alloy of 92% copper and 8% nickel.

Early this year the U.S. Mint announced that it had run out of silver bullion blanks, and is suspending the production of American Eagle Silver Proof coins until further notice.

In addition to being cut out of the minting process, silver will begin to show its true value in other ways. We are undoubtedly facing a great deal of inflation in the years ahead, which should cause untold numbers of people to begin accumulating precious metals as a hedge against inflation and a depressed dollar. Silver will play an important role in this hedging process.

The only real source of silver for new investment demand is silver already held as investment, namely, existing world inventories. In simple terms, since all newly produced silver is already spoken for by industry and fabrication demands, the only real silver available for new silver investors is the sale and resale of silver by existing silver investors who hold one or another form of silver and are willing to trade.

Increasing Investment Demand for Silver

One of the differences between silver and gold is that for over the lifetime of structural silver deficit (60+ years), there was very little, if any, net investment in silver while gold investment has increased dramatically over that time period. For silver, net investment has begun to change only in recent years.

It is precisely this shift in silver investing that signals the rebirth of silver as an investment asset. Potentially, increasing silver investments can be come to herald a quite bullish development in the world of precious metals.

Think of it - the world draws down and depletes silver inventory for more than 60 consecutive years, exhausting the very source of what is available for investment, and only then collectively decides that silver is a good investment.

Silver appears on the investment horizon precisely when there is less supply of the metal than ever before in history. Do you sense some profits on the horizon? I do.

Silver - Either Nearly Used Up or In the Landfill

It's true. 90 percent of all silver is used up in various industrial, manufacturing, and other processes. Most of the rest ends up in a landfill because it is considered valuable enough to recover. That will soon change.

Are you aware of the role silver plays in your everyday life? World consumption has never been higher - and for good reason. Here is just a brief list of some important uses of silver:

- Jewelry
- Electronic devices
- Silver oxide batteries
- Piping
- Water filtration
- Solar panels

A $100 dollar phone contains about 5 cents worth of silver as of late 2010. It costs more than that to retrieve it, even if the price goes up dramatically. But what about when that 5 cents is closer to a dollar?

The Internet has been a boon to small investors. Instant, uncensored communications and online trading have made more people aware of all kinds of investment opportunities. Silver is currently one such opportunity that merits serious consideration.

The Internet will ensure that the market for silver will be huge and that trading will be intense. Such is, of course, already the case, but it will be even more dynamic once the diminishing supply of silver begins to drive the market in a more realistic fashion than it has been allowed to do heretofore.

That the real story of silver remains largely unknown can be your powerful ally in the coming bull market for commodities. This story is one that more and more investors are bound to uncover in detail as time goes by.

Nothing Brings More Attention to an Investment Than Its Rising Price

For the past five years silver has recorded bigger price advances than gold, platinum and palladium. People are finally starting to take notice. Everyone likes it when things go up in value and silver has begun to catch the attention of investors all over the world.

Combine rising prices with a great investment story and you have the potential for an investment rush. This time it will the Great Silver Rush rather than the Gold Rush of generations past. It is time to stake your claim now.

We are in the very early stages of a long-term price boom in silver that will be caused by investment demand and low supply. The combination of an extremely small and tightly-held existing investment inventory, combined with a large potential investor base representing the the largest buying power in history, means countless investors who are hungry for the next hot investment and, for the time being at least, still unaware of the true story of silver as investment potential of unparalleled worth. It is the stuff that investment dreams are made of, the stuff that will make the savvy investors wealthy and the leave the reluctant ones broken and defeated.

Even thought the the price of silver has increased by more than 2-1/2 times in the past two years alone, the grey metal is still almost as cheap as dirt. Are you ready to take a chance to follow your own investment dream?

Is Sprott Physical Silver Trust The Better ETF Investment?

Silver has finally captured the investor attention that is so rightfully deserves. For years it languished in the shadow of its big brother gold.

But over the last few years, silver has staged an impressive run up that is actually greater than the more publicized gains in gold.

From its lows of 2010, the "other" precious metal silver has doubled in price through only the first quarter of 2011. The underlying supply and demand fundamentals of silver suggest that it will continue to rise over the next few years. You may wonder how you can effectively and economically gain exposure to silver.

In the past, you would have to go purchase physical silver bullion either in person, over the phone, or online, and then place it in a safe at home or a vault in a bank somewhere. Thanks to investment companies that have in recent years created silver ETF's, or Exchange Traded Funds, you do not have to do this any more.

There is one such silver ETF that offers differences from and advantages over other similar silver investment vehicles. In the following paragraphs, you will read about the pros and cons of the Sprott Physical Silver Trust and why it may be a good choice for your silver investments.

What is the Sprott Physical Silver Trust?

The Sprott physical silver trust is an exchange traded fund that you can buy individual units of on either the New York Stock Exchange ARCA or the TSX based in Toronto, Canada. Silver exchange traded funds have several things in common. They offer you the convenience to buy or sell your silver investments easily.

You do not have to take physical delivery of your silver, which means that you are not required to find a place to store it or pay to ship it when you are ready to sell part of it. This also provides you with a safety aspect, since you know that the exchange traded fund stores and protects your silver investment for you.

Silver ETF's like this one are extremely liquid investments. This means that you can buy or sell them with a few moments notice through your online broker account. Sprott physical silver trust provides all of these advantages that are typical of silver exchange traded funds.

How is the Sprott Physical Silver Trust Different from Other ETF's?

While the Sprott physical silver trust has many of the same features that make silver exchange traded funds popular with investors like yourself, it also has some important differences from them. With the other silver ETF's, the physical silver that the fund holds is not guaranteed to be fully in physical silver that is stored in a single, secure location.

Sprott guarantees that its silver bullion holdings are stored, segregated, and allocated by only the Royal Canadian Mint in Ottowa, Canada.

This storage facility is not merely a financial institution bank vault like the ones where other silver ETF's keep their silver bullion.

It is a Canadian government Crown corporation. The mint is responsible for any damage to or loss of the silver bullion. This silver is inspected routinely and audited annually in order to make sure that it is physically there in the quantity that the ETF states.

The fact that the Royal Canadian Mint keeps this silver physically present showcases another major distinction between Sprott physical silver trust and other silver exchange traded funds. Most precious metals ETF's keep their bullion in banks that loan out the silver to other parties who wish to borrow it. The Royal Canadian Mint does not ever loan out bullion that they keep in their vaults.

This means that your silver units investment is backed up by actual silver in the vaults, not by IOU's. The Sprott fund also does not settle for silver certificates that state that their silver is held in another mint or vault on their behalf. Other precious metals exchange traded funds will not make you this guarantee that the silver is physically present, accounted for, and can not be loaned out at all.

The Royal Canadian Mint is also the Sprott physical silver trust's counter party. This simply means that there is not another institution or company that stands in between you as a unit holder of this ETF and the silver holdings. You will find that many other precious metals ETF's do have such intermediary groups involved.

The more people that stand between you and your silver investment, the less secure it really is.

For American investors, Sprott physical silver trust also offers some substantial tax advantages.

Individual American holders of Sprott trust shares are able to realize lower capital gains rates of only fifteen percent on the sales of their silver investments.

This compares to a higher rate of typically twenty-eight percent capital gains taxes that the U.S. government levies on silver exchange traded funds based in the United States or actual silver coins that you sell. All that is required to take advantage of this lower tax rate is to hold the shares of the Sprott physical silver trust at least a year and to file a QEF form that they provide.

What Other Advantages Exist with the Sprott Physical Silver Trust Fund Shares?

The Sprott physical silver trust also allows you to redeem your shares in the fund for actual silver bars. You can do this on a once a month basis, although you must have a large holding of the securities.

Watch Eric Sprott on YouTube

If you own ten thousand ounces worth of units of the fund, then they will be happy to ship you the bars. This would be accomplished by an armored car transportation to almost any place in the world. When investors choose to exercise this option, the fund will make sure that the remaining share holders do not have their positions of silver diluted.

What Are the Disadvantages to the Sprott Physical Silver Trust Fund?

While this fund allows you to invest your money in shares that represent actual silver bullion for a lower price than if you go to purchase the physical silver yourself, this does not make it a completely perfect way to own silver for every investor.

Some of you may want the ability to get to your silver quickly in a severe economic crisis or national emergency. You are able to redeem your share units for actual silver with this fund, but this does not help you unless you have the ten thousand ounces worth of units of the fund. At $40 per ounce silver prices, this amounts to over $400,000 minimum for you to be able to take delivery of your actual silver.

There is also a small maintenance fee that is deducted against the value of the Sprott trust fund share units. It is less than half a percent a year of the shares' net asset value, or value of silver holdings per share.

If you can accept these few conditions of the Sprott Physical Silver Trust fund, it may be the best way for you to acquire and hold your silver investments. For those of you who want to hold the physical metal itself, you can always do this. For everyone else out there, can you think of a better way to have exposure to silver than this Sprott physical silver trust?

How Do Interest Rates Affect Your Investment Strategy?

When you are investing your hard earned money, you would like to get the best returns that you can with a manageable and tolerable degree of risk. One factor that plays a huge part in the returns on different types of investments is the interest rate.

Interest rates now remain at near historic lows. At some point, they will likely go up, whether the Fed raises them willingly or has its hand forced by higher inflation, or rising prices. High interest rates offer more advantages to various investments than do low interest rates.

In the subsequent paragraphs, you will begin to understand which investments are better in high interest rate and low interest rate environments.

Where Do You Invest When the Interest Rates are High?

As there is a great deal of speculation that interest rates will rise in the future, investments that do well with higher interest rates are a good place to start. Investments that revolve around interest rate yields, like bonds, invariably outperform in times of high interest rates.

Because bond prices are inversely related to the interest rates, high interest rates mean that bonds pay better yields, or returns, while their prices are low in comparison to the face value, or maturity day value, of the bond.

Once interest rates are already high, you might invest your money into longer maturity bonds to lock in the good rates. Just remember that the longer the time until a bond reaches maturity, the more sensitive its price will be to changes in rates along the way.

Longer Maturity Bonds Do Well With High Interest Rates

In a high interest rate environment, you can put money into bonds over stocks, since your chances to preserve your principal are often better with bonds. Stocks generally do not like high and rising interest rates, because this impacts companies' costs to borrow money and directly affects their profits.

High quality stocks that pay substantial dividends are an alternative place to invest your money in periods of high interest rates. Many quality companies will provide you with high dividend yields when the interest rates are greater in order to attract your investment away from Certificates of Deposit and bonds. With such stocks, you gain the double edged advantage of not only good current income, but also the possibility for the stock price to gain as the company appreciates in value over the long term.

Preferred stocks can also be good investments in times of high interest rates. Many preferred stocks will pay better yields than corporate bonds that have the same rating. Preferred stocks actually share more characteristics with bonds than stocks. You can buy them and sell them on the stock exchanges just like typical common stocks though.

If you are a more conservative investor, then you can also gain some type of return in times of high interest rates with money market accounts and certificates of deposit. In periods of high interest rates, you can gain five to ten percent returns and occasionally greater with these investments. You should shop around for the best possible rates in times of very high interest rates.

Where Do You Invest When the Interest Rates Are Low?

Today's interest rates definitely qualify as low. The truth is that at from 0 to .25%, the interest rates set by the Federal Reserve are as low as they have ever been before. This disadvantages bonds, certificates of deposit, money markets, and many preferred stocks that have fixed interest rates. Rates can hardly go lower, and as they rise, bond prices will decline.

Stocks Perform Better With Low Interest Rates

There are a few places that you can look for better returns in the low interest rate climate of today. Stocks are one such place. Stocks tend to perform well when interest rates are lower as companies are able to borrow money and expand with lower interest expenses. Some of the safer and surer types of stocks are utility stocks.

A great number of utilities are as solid as companies come in their finances, and they pay good dividend yields too. Some of these pay out around five percent dividends per year. They also tend to appreciate in value over time as their performances are quite consistent. Consolidated Edison of New York is one such utility.

Oil and Gas Trusts Do Well With Low Interest Rates

Oil pipeline master limited partnerships also offer possibilities for higher returns when interest rates are low. These entities make significant profits and pay them out to the investors each and every year. The yields on these are commonly six to seven percent and have been as high as ten to twelve percent. You also do not have to pay taxes on such master limited partnerships until the point that you decide to sell them.

Oil and gas trusts, such as the popular Canadian Oil and Gas Trusts, are another good place to look for higher returns when interest rates remain low. These companies own properties that produce oil and natural gas, as their name implies. They sell these products and disperse all of the profits that remain after operating expenses and new acquisitions.

Yields that run from eight to twelve percent are not uncommon with these entities. These are a far cry better than the near zero percent interest rates that you can get with many fixed income investments today.

If you feel like you must hold on to bonds in low interest rate periods, then you should stick with short term bonds. The prices on these instruments do not change much even when interest rates rise. When you hold the bond until it matures, then you do not have to worry about any changes in the price of the bond, as you would have to with a stock. This will at least provide you with peace of mind that riskier investments might not.

Cooperate Bonds and Emerging Market Bonds

If you are simply looking for a good place to park your money for a while until better opportunities arise, this is one investment that you might consider. It will not make you a wonderful return, but short term corporate bonds, high yield investment grade bonds, or emerging market bonds will provide you with a significantly better return than savings accounts and certificates of deposit do.

Is it Possible to Predict the Change in Interest Rates?Now at this point, you may be thinking that it would certainly be helpful if there were only a way to predict changes in interest rates. The good news is that since interest rates in the U.S. are set by the Federal Reserve, much of the time you can make such predictions.

Listen to the Federal Reserve Statements

The Federal Reserve holds periodic meetings where they discuss the economic situation in the U.S. and give indications as to what their monetary policy on interest rates will be in the future. If you listen carefully to these statements that they issue, you will be able to pick up on what their future moves are likely to be.

Many investment services also put out their interpretation and analysis of if and when the Fed will raise or lower interest rates. There are even investments in the market that give out a percentage chance that the Fed will raise or lower interest rates by a given month.

Use all of the information sources that are freely available to you, and you will be surprised at how well that you can anticipate changes in Fed policy that will lead to higher or lower interest rates in the near and medium term future.

Protect Your 401K Investment From These Two Threats

You may be like the majority of Americans who now rely on a combination of social security and 401K investments in order to plan for their retirement future. In recent months, you have probably heard that the future of social security is now in debate.

At the very least, there will be cuts to benefits and later retirement ages mandated in the future. Your 401K is something that you believe will be there to help you achieve retirement. Although you may not have heard much about this yet, there are also big problems with your 401k.

The subsequent paragraphs will show you how the damage to your 401k is already evident, even though you do not hear about it yet on the financial news.

Inflation is Rising

Inflation is a threat that you mostly think and hear about when you do your shopping. In food prices, gas stations, and now even clothing prices, you see and feel that your dollars do not stretch as far as they used to even a year or two ago. This is a result of inflation, or a rise in the prices of goods and services.

The revered economist Milton Friedman taught that inflation is always an event that is driven when government creates and prints money. You may not be aware of this, but the government through the Federal Reserve has been steadily eroding your dollar's purchasing power over the years.

Almost every year, they expand the amount of dollars in circulation when they electronically print money and pass it on to banks to loan out in multiples of the amounts that banks keep on deposit, or their reserve ratios.

How High Is Inflation Officially?

The government publishes an official measure of inflation called the CPI, or consumer price index. It measures changes in the prices of various goods and assigns certain weights to the different components. In the early 1980's inflation reached an average of over 13.5% for just the year 1980.

The Chairman of the Federal Reserve Paul Volcker managed to beat it down by raising interest rates to over 18%. Inflation then declined to a more manageable level for the rest of the decade. Since 1990, inflation has officially averaged pretty much between two and six percent per year.

The numbers for 2011 have come out in the two and a half percent range so far. This may not sound like a lot, but it adds up over time. Over the last twenty years, inflation has totaled over seventy-one percent according to these CPI numbers. This means that you need at least one hundred and seventy-one dollars now to buy something that only cost you one hundred dollars in 1990.

How High Is Inflation Actually?

To disguise the actual level of inflation, the Bureau of Labor Statistics that puts out the inflation numbers has radically changed the way that it counts inflation in the years since this peaked in the fourteen percent range in the early 1980's. They have done this in the name of accounting for quality improvements and product substitution.

One organization called Shadow Government Statistics keeps an honest track of inflation according to the way that the BLS initially measured it. If you figure up inflation using the methodology that was in place before 1980, then in February of 2011 you saw inflation reach 9.6% on an annual basis.

This is almost four times the amount of the official CPI numbers that the government releases now. Even if you go back to the way that they figured the CPI formula before 1990, you would still have an inflation rate of 5.5% and climbing.

At these higher real inflation rates, you would have inflation of over a hundred percent in the last twenty years.

Why Is Inflation a Threat to Your 401K Value?

You can already see how inflation that officially totaled over seventy-one percent and really from one to two hundred percent over the last twenty years has drastically affected your ability to buy things. Where you may not have made the inflation threat connection is with your 401k value.

The ability of your 401k money and income that it produces to purchase necessary goods and services is critical when you go onto a fixed income in retirement. Imagine if you had retired in 1990 and were still attempting to live off of your 401k income today.

If you were receiving a thousand dollars a month in 1990 from this income, then you would need seventeen hundred dollars a month in 2011 just to have the same standard of living that you possessed at the opening of the 1990's. It is highly unlikely that your investments would be generating this much more income now than they did back then.

This means that the difference would either have to come from you taking money from your retirement account each month to cover the shortfall, or you would have to work a part time job to keep up with costs.

These calculations have again only considered the lower inflation picture that the government has officially reported in the last two decades. Thanks to the government choosing to spend without restraint and to wildly print money since 2007, even low official inflation rates of a few percent a year can no longer be taken for granted.

At some point, inflation will be as high again as it was in the early 1980's. The future purchasing power of your 401k could easily be less than half of what it is now in twenty years from today.

Is the Government Itself Another Future Threat to Your 401K?

There is a new threat to the value of your 401K in the wake of the financial crisis that has caused the U.S. government to run unprecedented deficits. The U.S. public debt now stands at over fourteen trillion dollars.

The credit rating of the U.S. government has been put on negative outlook by S&P in April of 2011. If the government reaches the point where its over one hundred and twenty year duration top credit rating is downgraded and there are not enough buyers for its critical bonds from the usual overseas customers, then they may have to nationalize the 401K plans and convert your investments into government bonds to substitute for the lost buyers.

You have seen other countries around the world resort to these types of measures in crises before. You should not believe that the U.S. government is incapable of these actions as it grows increasingly desperate to finance its runaway spending and debt. The problem with these bonds is that they would not be worth anything at this point, and neither would your retirement investments.

How Can You Protect Your 401K Investments from these Threats?

The safest and surest way to protect your 401K investments from these two threats of inflation and government seizure is to withdraw the funds from the government plans altogether. You would take a hit of up to 30% in penalties, but it would allow you to gain full control over your money. Once you did this, you might divide it into two halves and place the first half in gold and the second in silver.

Over the long haul, the two precious metals have always kept pace with and often exceeded inflation. In the long term bull market that we are in for gold and silver, they are likely to continue to outperform other traditional investments such as the stock market, as they have since the year 2000.

Would it not be better to suffer a thirty percent penalty now and gain the chance for your money to appreciate massively in value than to watch it be slowly eaten away by inflation or taken by the government in the future?

Why Silver Will Get More Volatile With Higher Prices

The first week of May saw silver rapidly give up much of the incredible gains it had consistently made for several consecutive months since the beginning of 2011. If you had just acquired your position in silver in the forty to almost fifty dollar range, then you suddenly found yourself underwater on the investment.

This should not cause you to lose faith in silver as a viable medium to long term holding. Gold also declined, but not at nearly the rate that silver did. There are a number of reasons why silver prices are so much more volatile than gold. In the paragraphs that follow, you will learn why silver prices seem to be unstable and will get even more volatile at higher levels.

How Much Did Silver Decline the First Week of May?

Silver certainly took the old stock market adage to sell in May and go away seriously. After making a three decade high the last trading day of April, the metal plunged much of the first week of May. The other precious metal, as analysts sometimes call silver, dropped over twenty-seven percent from its high the week before.

One of the trading days alone, it even fell an eye popping ten percent. This violent move back down caused a chain reaction of events that only served to make the sell off worse. Traders who had bought silver on margin, or borrowed money, had to sell off either some of their silver positions or other assets in order to come up with more margin money. This caused other commodities, such as oil and copper, to drop along with silver.

What Caused Silver to Drop So Steeply?

You will not find one single reason for why silver declined so sharply the first week of May. The simplest answer is that several larger silver investors decided to sell a large portion of their holdings on high prices and news. Bin Laden the feared Al Qaeda terrorist leader was killed over that first weekend of May.

George Soros the famed commodities and currency investor decided to take profits. Besides this Hungarian born investor, the wealthiest man on the planet Carlos Slim also started to sell his positions. Naturally, when word of this leaked out, it sparked a panic among other nervous silver investors who did not want to go against the so called smart money.

Silver was also affected by a perceived slow down or even future down turn in the world economy. Economic data that the government released around the first week of May showed that the U.S. economic growth has slowed considerably and the unemployment rate has risen again. As silver is as much an industrial use metal as it is an investment metal, this clouded the industrial demand picture for the white metal in the short term.

A lesser known reason also emerged to dampen silver's soaring prospects the first week of May. The Chicago Mercantile Exchange Group is the largest commodities exchange operator in the world. They began to move to cut down on speculation in commodities in April and May. In fact, the CME raised its margin requirements for silver positions five different times in the prior several weeks.

With each higher margin requirement setting, it became more expensive for investors to hold large speculative silver positions that they did not actually buy outright with cash. Since the amount of required silver margin tripled in the last month, investors need three times as much money in their accounts to hold the same amount of silver positions.

Where you only had to post three percent of the value of a silver contract in early April, now you must put up more than nine percent. You would have to pay over twenty-one thousand dollars to hold a five thousand ounce contract of silver.

Why Had Silver Risen So Dramatically?

Silver had risen over eighty percent in the preceding months since the end of 2010. This is an enormous run even for silver. The white metal soared this time mostly because of its properties as an alternative currency and safe haven investment. In the past, silver has functioned as much as a currency as has gold.

As the Federal Reserve has continued to make money available easily and to electronically print it, fears have risen that these policies will cause inflation. Silver has been priced so much more cheaply than gold that many investors believe it is a more affordable place to keep their money to protect it from perceived inflation.

As the Fed's policies have weakened the dollar, silver has also benefited and risen inversely. The low interest rates and incredible liquidity that are the results of these programs also have boosted silver's value.

What Makes Silver So Much More Volatile Than Gold?

You may still not understand why silver's rise and fall has to be so dramatic. After all, gold moves up and down too, but not in such shocking amounts as ten percent at a single time. The main difference between silver and gold is the size of the markets. There is sixteen times as much gold in the world as there is silver.

The silver market is actually incredibly tiny. Deutsche Bank says that the entire world wide demand for silver is around a billion ounces. Most of this demand comes from the silver Exchange Traded Funds. This puts a tremendous strain on the available silver when demand is high. The end result is that prices can be very easily forced higher when significant demand comes into the market.

Similarly, if a number of large silver positions are dumped at once, prices can plummet. Higher prices are a sign that there is not enough silver to go around. Unfortunately, silver does not become more readily available just because prices are rising. Instead, it only makes the prices still more volatile.

Why Will Silver Rebound from these Intense Price Corrections?

For those of you who invested in silver late in the most recent run, you do not have to panic about the price correction. This is because silver is likely to return to the $50 level again even this year. The fundamental reasons for the rise of silver have not changed.

Many investors who sold out near the highs are only waiting for it to return to the low to mid thirty dollar support levels of the metal before they buy their positions back. They know that they could easily pick up fifty percent price gains from these levels, now that a new multiple decade high of nearly $50 has been set.

Another reason that silver is likely to rebound is because analysts expect gold prices to continue to rise. Silver almost always moves in the same direction as gold. This is a historical trend that goes back thousands of years. In the past, silver averaged a sixteen to one price ratio to gold.

At the current prices of gold around $1,500 per ounce, that would have silver fairly valued at more than $90 per ounce. Remember that the inflation adjusted highs for the silver prices of the early 1980's is more than $120 per ounce in today's dollars. With all of this in mind, does fifty dollar silver sound overvalued to you?

More details about silver in my new book: Building Wealth with Silver

Low Income Apartments - A Better Real Estate Investment?

If you are an investor in houses or rental properties then you will be concerned with the housing market's performance these days. Despite the much lauded economic recovery that is supposed to be underway, the latest news on the U.S. housing market front will not inspire property investors.

Read on to learn why home prices are still falling and what areas of residential real estate continue to make the most sense for your investment dollars today.

Why Are Housing Prices Still Falling?

New reports in May from two real estate tracking firms Clear Capital and Zillow.com show that the hoped for bottom in the housing market has not yet appeared. In fact, housing prices have entered an official double dip on a national basis. Clear Capital shows that these average national home prices are now below the former Great Recession lows of March 2009.

You might be mystified as to how this could happen. The problem lies with the foreclosed properties and short sales that banks continue to move to sell. Bank owned property sales have reached a shocking 34.5% of the entire housing market. This has caused the nation's average home price to decline by 4.9% for the quarter and five percent on a year on year basis.

The home prices for the country have actually dropped by 11.5% over the past nine months leading up to May 2011. This rate of decline has not been witnessed since 2008, back in the worst part of the financial meltdown and crisis.

The foreclosed property sales were hard enough on home prices, but now short sales that allow borrowers to sell and walk away from houses on which they are underwater are exerting a larger negative force on the market. Zillow.com reported May 9th that there is now an all time high of homeowners who have negative equity in their property, or who owe more than their property is worth.

Negative Equity Has Risen to 28.4%

This number of negative equity home owners has risen to 28.4% of all single family houses that have a mortgage. If your property is in one of the major metropolitan area's then the numbers are higher. In Atlanta the negative equity home owners are 55.7%, in Chicago they are about 46%, in Denver they are 41%, in Massachusetts they are 46%, and in Phoenix it is almost 75%.

This information comes with both good news and bad news. The good news is that the foreclosures on new mortgages are significantly lower than on the ones made before the housing and financial crisis. The bad news is that at the rate the banks are going, they will require a good four years more to work through all of the defaulted loans that will go to foreclosure. This means that it will take them longer still to sell the houses on the real estate market.

Another reason that home prices continue to fall is that the availability of mortgages remains scarce. This is particularly the case for middle to lower income borrowers. Consumer confidence in this housing market is already weak. This all leads to a vicious cycle where prices continue to fall and your chances of being underwater on your properties increase.

What Do the Falling Home Prices Mean for Your Investment?

It is clear that lower prices on primary and investment properties are here to stay for a while. You should not count on a higher year end to the value of your investment properties in 2011. Remember that these losses are only on paper unless you have to sell them. In the meanwhile, you can continue or start to rent out your property and have a nice stream of income that comes in to cover the mortgage and provide additional cash flow each month.

Where Should You Invest in Residential Real Estate Now?

While home prices continue to fall, it is dangerous to invest in single family homes and even townhouses. Eventually, you will see a bottom, but it may not be until after your new purchases are underwater. There are other areas of the real estate market where you can invest and still make money, even as prices decline.

Low income apartments are a good investment even in this challenging real estate market. This is because people will always need low cost housing. When you buy or build apartments for low income families, you can expect to receive a good return on your money. These are long term investments that will not cost you so much per unit and will allow you to wait out the price changes in housing.

In the meanwhile, you will have more money come in than the mortgage payment that will allow you to have additional income even while you are paying off the property. This rental income can last for many years if you keep up the maintenance on the apartments.

As an example, you might realize eight hundred dollars in rent on a town house that costs you around $130,000 in a small town. Low income apartments in such a town might cost you around $50,000 per unit but will still rent for five hundred dollars.

Townhouses Versus Rental Apartment Unit

The townhouse is more than two and a half times as much money to buy as the low rental apartment unit, but it does not pay even twice as much rent. Units that cost you so much less upfront return a disproportionate amount of rent for the cost of the property and mortgage payments.

This provides a greater amount of cash flow as you are able to acquire more rental units for the same money as the higher priced properties. They also are lower valued units that will not decline as sharply in value as other more expensive townhouses and single family homes. This is what makes low income apartments such strong investments in this real estate climate and any housing market.

There are also tax advantages that you gain with low income apartments. Most municipalities, states, and even the federal government will provide you with tax credits when you own and rent out low income apartments. You are also able to write off expenses with upkeep and maintenance. Using these credits, the income that you realize on the venture can be almost tax free.

It is true that there can be more work when you own low income apartments. You may have to stay on top of your tenants to get the rent on time, and it may be paid late more often than with a higher end tenant in a more expensive property. You will probably have some small repairs to contend with too. These are all part of the reasons that your rate of rent return is higher on low income apartments than on traditional townhouses and houses.

What Residential Properties Should You Not Invest In?

As you look around for real estate to not get trapped in, there are certain types that you should definitely avoid. Any area, city, and especially neighborhood that features a great number of foreclosures is dangerous. These properties may boast attractive prices, but they are likely to come down further still.

You also want to avoid properties in areas where the unemployment rate is higher than the national average. It will be difficult for property prices to be sustained and recover where the job base is not there to support new home purchases. Is it not better to err on the side of caution where real estate investments are concerned in the double dip housing market that we have entered?

How to Invest in Commodities with Exchange Traded Funds

Over the last year, you have watched the prices of natural resources skyrocket. This has probably grabbed your attention. You may have found yourself wishing that you could become involved with investments in commodities as they soared.

In the past, this type of investment required complicated futures and options that you purchased on commodities exchanges. The entry barriers kept out novice to intermediate investors most of the time.

This has all changed in the last few years thanks to the advent of Commodities Exchange Traded Funds. In the paragraphs below, you will learn what these Commodities ETF's are and how easy it is for you to start to invest in them.

What Are Commodities Exchange Traded Funds?

Commodities ETF's are exchange traded funds that operate much like a mutual fund. The main difference is that they do not have much in the way of management. This works to your benefit, since there are lower expense ratios than with mutual funds.

Commodity ETF's possess defined investment plans in one or more resources that can be altered from time to time by the manager of the fund. These particular ETF's allow you to get involved in commodities' markets and provide you with a terrific way to diversify your investments.

ETF's based on commodities were designed to mimic the performance of commodities. They do this by purchasing futures contracts on their underlying respective commodities in the futures exchanges. These ETF's are easy to own, since they can be traded over stock exchanges. This means that you can purchase or sell them whenever you want in market trading hours, just like a stock.

A tremendous advantage that commodities exchange traded funds offer you is that you are not able to lose more than the money that you put into the ETF, as you could by directly trading the futures markets themselves.

What Types of Commodities Exchange Traded Funds Exist?

In general, commodities ETF's can be broken down into two categories, those that invest in a basket of multiple resources versus those that pick only one resource in which to invest. If you are an investor who is not sure which commodity will outperform over time, then the entire commodities index ETF's are the way to go.

These types of ETF's offer you better diversification for your portfolio. If you are someone who has a strong opinion on precious metals like gold and silver, agriculture like wheat and corn, or energies like oil and natural gas, then you should consider these individual resource ETF's instead.

The fact remains that the most popular commodities ETF's are those that buy into various resources. There are typically five categories of commodities in which they invest. These include agriculture, energy, precious metals, industrial metals, and livestock. Each of these have their own characteristics and appeal.

Agriculture and energy resources often experience tremendous volatility in prices because of disruptions to supply. Precious metals enjoy enormous appeal for their safe haven status. Industrial metals mostly move up and down in correlation to the world wide demand for such raw materials.

What Specific Multiple Commodities Exchange Traded Funds Are Available?

In the category of broad based commodities basket ETF's, there are a number of them out there. Five of these represent the more popular ones that you might select. Each of them has their own particular natures.

GSP is the S&P GSCI Total Return Index offered by iPath. It follows an index that contains almost seventy percent contracts in energy futures. This means that it is heavily weighted towards natural gas, Brent crude oil, WTI oil, and heating oil. It only contains a three percent exposure to precious metals.

Livestock makes up under five percent of its assets. Naturally, this ETF will appeal to you if you believe heavily in energy price appreciation but also wish for a small exposure to the other resource commodities.

DJP is another option for baskets of commodities. The Dow Jones-AIG Commodity Index is also brought to you by i-Path.

The commodities in this index tracker are adjusted on an annual basis. No sub category in resources may make up more than thirty-three percent of the total. Energy is still the most significant component, but this is only by a matter of percentage points rather than being the overwhelming majority of the fund's assets.

A third popular choice is the **GSG**, or S&P GSCI Commodity-Indexed Trust, offered by iShares. It tracks the Goldman Sachs Commodities Index. Twenty-four various commodities are included in it. Even so, it also has a heavy bias towards energy with more than two thirds of the assets comprised of energies. The components are added up to match the importance of each commodity to the overall global economy. With over two billion in assets, it is one of the larger multiple resource ETF's available to you.

DBC is a fourth possibility for you. Offered by PowerShares, the DB Commodity Index Tracking Fund follows the results of the Deutsche Bank Liquid Commodity Index. The resources in this index include crude oil, heating oil, gold, aluminum, wheat, and corn. This represents one of the lowest varieties of holdings among commodities funds. You should be comfortable with these six different commodities before you invest in it.

Finally you have the **GCC**, known as the GreehHaven Continuous Commodity Fund. This offers you better diversification than the heavy bias towards energy that most of the other commodities ETF's favor. It provides you with an equal weighting comprising seventeen different commodities. This means that energies only make up around eighteen percent of the overall holdings.

It has a significant bias towards agriculture, so this is a better choice for those of you who believe in higher agriculture prices. Grains comprise eighteen percent of the total, and livestock accounts for twelve percent. Coffee, cotton, cocoa, sugar, and orange juice make up about thirty percent of the holdings. At over forty percent of agricultural commodities positions, you should believe strongly in them to buy into this fund.

What Are Some of the More Popular Individual Commodities Exchange Traded Funds?

Others of you may have specific ideas on which individual resources that you want to pursue. For you, individual commodities ETF's may be more appropriate. Five of the various resources have popular ETF's based on their changes in price and performance. One of the best known of these today is **GLD**, the popular gold based **SPDR** Gold Trust Shares.

For those of you who believe that silver has more potential to move up significantly in price percentage, there is the **SLV** iShares silver trust silver based ETF. The aptly named symbol OIL offers you the S&P GSCI's Crude Oil Total Return Index. If you favor natural gas price improvements, you can always look into the **UNG**, or United States Natural Gas ETF.

A good way to play a global economic recovery is to invest in copper, the world's foremost industrial metal that is a barometer for global expansion. You can do this with the ETF **JJC**, the **AIG** Copper Total Return fund that is offered by iPath Dow Jones.

Commodities are in a long term bull market that still has years left to run. How much longer will you wait to invest in scarce resources that are in ever increasing demand?

How to Protect Your Stocks With An Option Insurance

If you invest money in the stock market, then chances are good that you spend a lot of time thinking or even worrying about how low your investments may sink if the markets drop again. This is a natural fear after the shocking declines in the stock market that you witnessed just a few years ago.

The good news is that you do not have to be afraid of your investments in stocks. There is a form or insurance that you can take out on most stocks called options. In the paragraphs that follow, you will learn why you need options insurance and how it can protect your investments from declines in the market.

What is the Potential Problem with the Stock Market?

There are many reasons that you could be justified in your fears of a potential fall in the stock markets. This is historically the time of year when many investors sell in May and go away until October or November.

While it has not happened every year, it has occurred often enough for many investors to choose to take their profits in May. This is especially the case after there have been significant gains like we have seen the first four months of the year.

Many analysts will also tell you that we are long overdue for a significant ten percent correction in stock prices. The market has rallied a long way off of the 2008 lows. Markets can not only move in one direction in a straight line. Corrections of ten percent and more are healthy and necessary.

This could put a significant dent in the value of your stock portfolio.

You might also have heard financial television pundits discuss an eerie resemblance between the stock market recovery patterns following the 1929 start of the Great Depression and the 2008 Great Recession. What would happen to the value of your stocks if the market in 2011 took a nose dive off the cliff as they did a second time in 1932 when many thought that the worst of the Great Depression had already passed?

As you saw in the troubled years of 2007 and 2008, the lowest that a stock price can decline to is zero. The good news is that you do not have to fret over these very real possibilities. You can obtain options insurance and rest easy at night when you know that your stock investment principal is one hundred percent protected.

What Can You Do About A Potential Stock Market Drop?

You would not drive a car without auto insurance. Given the choice, you would not go about your daily activities without life insurance and health insurance. There is no reason to put your hard earned money into investments that can lose one hundred percent of their value and not have investment insurance. This is where options on stocks come into play. When you own insurance on your stocks, you do not have to care about a stock market decline.

What Is Option Insurance?

Options are literally contracts that give you the right to buy or sell a stock at a certain price, the strike price, by a particular date, the expiration date. When you purchase a call option, you gain the opportunity to buy a stock at the options' strike price up to the point that the option expires.

When you purchase a put option, you obtain the opportunity to sell the stock at that contract's strike price up to the day of expiration. For you who own stocks and are seeking insurance against price declines, it is the put option contracts that you are interested in buying.

The cost of these insurance put options is known as the premium, as it is with other forms of insurance. When you buy a put or call option, the only money that you have at risk is this premium. This premium that you pay is the cost to obtain your put option insurance on your stocks.

How Does Option Insurance Work?

Options have a particular set of rules that they follow. Each option contract represents one hundred shares of the underlying stock. You will see that stock options trade with strike prices that run in intervals of $2.50 on stock prices up to $30 and in intervals of $5 for stocks priced over $30.

Options with strike prices near the actual price of the stock are pretty heavily traded and readily available to you. Those options with strike prices far away from the actual price of the stock are harder to obtain, but you would not require those for your insurance purposes anyway.

Stock options do expire on a set date. This is known as the expiration date. You can obtain your options insurance with typical options for up to nine months. If you wish to insure your stocks for longer, you can by LEAPS, or long term options, that come with expiration dates as far as three years away from the present date.

The key to remember when you insure your stocks with put options is that you want to buy a put contract with a strike price at or as close to your purchase price of the stock as possible. This way, if the stock declines in value below your purchase price, the writer of your put option will be forced to take your shares of stock at the price that you paid for them. In other words, you will get your investment principal back in exchange for giving the writer or seller of the option your stock shares.

An example For How This Works Out In Practice

If you own shares of Citibank that you bought at forty dollars per share, you want to make sure that the price does not decline below this forty dollars. So you simply place an order to buy one put option contract for every one hundred shares of Citibank stock that you own.

You will have to decide how long you want your stock insurance for, as you can have it for one month, several months, or even one to three years. Naturally, you will pay more money for a longer amount of time on the option, but it will work out to be a smaller amount of money per month if you buy a longer option.

For example, six month options are less expensive per month than one or two months options are. Most reasonable of all are the LEAPS options where your per month cost basis becomes considerably less.

As a real world example, when Citibank was trading at $41.35 on May 19, the June 18 Puts at 40 strike price cost $55 to insure your one hundred shares, almost fourteen percent per year. The July 16 Puts are only $105, a cost of just over $50 per month.

The September 17 Puts were going for $180, or $45 per month. January 21, 2012 Puts are only $300, a price of $37.50 a month, around nine and a half percent per year. January 19, 2013 Puts are $570, which is only $28.50 per month, or about seven and a half percent a year.

When the prices for complete peace of mind are so reasonable, why would you not want to insure your stock portfolio?

5 Reasons Why Silver Investments Outperform Gold

These days, every where you turn you hear financial channel talking heads and economic analysts extolling the virtues of investing in gold.

Between inflation threats, instability in the Middle East, financial troubles in the Euro Zone, and the teetering on the brink of double dip recession American economy, there are plenty of good reasons for the recommendation to buy the yellow metal that acts as a protective hedge against all of these threatening events.

What you may not know is that silver offers similar protection against such instability and economic chaos at a fraction of the price per ounce of gold. There are five main reasons why silver turns out to be a superior investment over gold that you will learn about in the following paragraphs.

1. Silver is Actually Rarer than Gold Today

The available stocks of silver bullion are less than are the readily available stocks of gold. The World Gold Council states that as many as four to five billion ounces of physical gold are still present in the world.

This is the case with gold since the most famous of precious metals is almost never used up; instead it is recycled from time to time from jewelry to coins to bars.

Ninety-five percent of the gold ever mined in the history of the world is still above ground somewhere in a bank vault, coin shop, government hoard, or individual's home.

Contrast these gold supply fundamentals with silver. As of the World Silver Survey in 2004, only six hundred and seventy-one million usable silver ounces existed above ground with which to meet world demand.

By the end of 2009, the above ground usable silver stocks had dropped to twenty million ounces. Even if you account for the greater investment demand for gold over silver today, the supply side of the equation tells you that silver should be worth far more than the $35 to $37 per ounce range where it trades these days, especially when gold is over $1,540 per ounce.

2. Silver is 90% Used Up by Consumer Goods And Stored in Land Fills

You may raise your eyebrows at the incredible suggestion that ninety percent of silver is used up in and lost with consumer goods today. As these consumer goods are disposed of, the silver goes to the land fill with them. When did silver become a disposable commodity? It began only a few years after the end of the second world war.

Industrial applications for silver have progressively grown since the 1940's until ten thousand different applications for the metal have been found.

The overwhelming majority of these see the silver used and then discarded with the television sets, photographs, batteries, hospital equipment, clothing, wiring, catheters, and so forth.

In fact, a staggering four hundred and fifty-five million plus ounces of silver that are mined each year go into these industrial products. Another one hundred and twenty-eight million ounces of silver are used in film production and developing. Another nearly sixty million ounces are designated to become silverware that decorates tables, drawers, and china cabinets around the world.

Only a hundred and sixty-three million silver ounces actually go into jewelry. The costly process of recovering and recycling silver simply does not make sense at the low silver prices on the world market. Since over ninety percent of all silver mined goes directly into industrial applications and consumer products, this makes silver a far better investment today than gold that is mostly used and re-used for coins, jewelry, and bars.

3. Silver is in Greater Demand than Gold

You have to understand the difference between simply investment demand and total demand. There is no doubt that gold is in greater investment demand than is silver by far. But because of its myriads of uses for industrial needs, consumer products, medical devices and equipment, silverware, and photography, silver is in significantly greater demand than gold overall.

More gold is mined each day than is needed by the world investment communities. For many years, a smaller amount of silver has been mined than is actually utilized. This puts silver in a supply and demand deficit that dates back to 1942.

So while there may be enough gold to satisfy investor demand for the precious metal most of the time, silver is constantly drawing down on the usable world silver reserves.

As you will see in the next point, these reserves have run from enormous levels seventy years ago to dangerously low levels today.

4. Silver Production and Inventories Are Down

You can see how enormous an impact the silver supply and demand imbalance has created when you look at the history of world available silver stocks going back to the 1940's. At the conclusion of World War II, the world silver stocks amounted to ten billion ounces.

An incredible four billion of these ounces, forty percent of world holdings, lay securely in the vaults of the U.S. government. Now there are approximately twenty million ounces of spare usable silver available in world stockpiles.

Today, the U.S. government has so few ounces in its reserves that it has to halt production of American silver eagles from time to time, not because it can not keep up with demand, but because it lacks the silver bullion to produce the blanks required for coinage.

Not only are silver inventories at shockingly low levels today as compared to gold, but silver possesses among the lowest ratios of reserves to production and the smallest reserve base to production ratio.

You can not argue with the fact that silver is the closest of all the commercially mined metals to actually reaching Hubert's Peak, better known in pop culture by the name of peak production. When this point occurs, silver will see a smaller and smaller quantity of production every year than in the years before, since fully half of the silver reserves in existence below ground will have been brought to light.

The half of the silver that remains in the earth will only be located in more remote locations of the earth and in deeper places that are harder to reach. The silver that is mined in the future will be produced at prices that rise over time, according to the reality of peak silver production.

5. The Historical Silver to Gold Ratio

Throughout past history, silver has always existed at around twelve times the abundance of gold. This lead to a silver price of one twelfth that of gold. In point of fact, this relationship between gold and silver was a stable twelve to one throughout most of recorded human history.

At the world market prices today, gold is forty-two times more expensive than silver per ounce. This argues for sharply higher silver prices at some point in the future, even if gold does not go up any higher in the years to come. Based on the mid $1,500 per ounce price of gold these days, silver should reach a level approaching one hundred and thirty dollar per ounce at some point.

In light of these critical revelations about silver, which of the two precious metals would you prefer to own for the maximum price appreciation potential?

Gold And Silver Restrictions For Americans Are Coming

Over the last few months, you may have heard of some stiff new financial regulations that the United States is implementing as of mid July. These new regulations are called the Frank-Dodd Reform Act.

While there are many provisions of this bill that are designed to protect Americans from the greedy and malicious actions that large banks and hedge funds performed on the U.S. and world economy, others will limit your investment abilities and freedoms.

In particular, your ability to trade gold and silver is about to be severely restricted if you reside within the U.S. In the following paragraphs, you will learn what the Frank-Dodd Reform Act is, how it will affect gold and silver purchase prices, who it applies to, and what impacts this will have on the prices of gold and silver.

What is the Frank-Dodd Reform Act?

The Frank-Dodd Reform Act is an American federal statute that became law when the democratically controlled congress and President Barack Obama collaborated together. The law is intended to enact a series of reforms in financial regulations within the U.S.

It alters the present day regulatory regimes for a wide variety of financial and banking markets and institutions. You will see some new agencies created and others eliminated or merged so that the regulatory process can be streamlined.

There are several purposes of this act. It establishes greater oversight of institutions that act as a risk to the financial system. It will encourage transparency in markets, and it will amend the Federal Reserve Act.

These new supervisions and standards are intended to safeguard American consumers, businesses, investors and the overall economy. They are to put a stop to financial institution bailouts that tax payers provide. The act also creates an early alert system on the stability of the economy and the financial institutions. Besides this, it establishes rules concerning executive pay and how corporations can be governed.

Loopholes in the financial system and markets that made the Great Recession possible are supposed to be eliminated by all of this. The act has many noble goals but includes a huge amount of restrictions that will not be so good for the economy and investors. Among the two hundred and forty-three different rules that it requires regulators to establish is one that will severely limit your ability to trade gold and silver.

How Does It Affect Gold and Silver Purchases?

If you are an investor who likes to trade gold and silver, you will soon see that you are at odds with one of the provisions in the Frank-Dodd Reform Act. This new restriction is summed up in a recent decision that Forex.com, one of the main forex trading outfits in the U.S., made and wrote about to all of their trader clients.

Because of the Frank-Dodd Reform Act that is coming into effect on Friday, July 15, 2011, Forex.com believes that U.S. residents will no longer be able to trade precious metals like silver and gold over the counter anymore. To this effect, they are *not going to permit their American residents to trade any metals anymore come July 15th*.

ZeroHedge and LeapRate first picked up on this announcement that has caused a great deal of controversy. Does the new ruling mean that you can no longer buy and sell gold and silver in the United States? Forex.com is clearly interpreting this new act as a ban that prohibits American residents to trade either gold or silver contracts.

The Frank-Dodd Reform Act does allow for one exemption in retail precious metals transactions. Silver and gold can still be purchased, so long as they are delivered to the customer in twenty-eight days or less. This means that you can still buy physical gold and silver and take possession of it. But since you must physically have it in under a month, you can not trade futures or Forex contracts on gold and silver that allow you to leverage your dollars, or multiply your money to buy far larger amounts of gold and silver than your money will actually purchase.

The goal in this was not to keep small investors from the gold and silver trade. The legislation is aimed at hedge fund managers who trade enormous quantities of precious metals and other complex leveraged financial instruments. These groups have the power to move and destabilize such markets with devastating results. Still, it does restrict small investors like you all the same, since you will no longer be able to engage in speculative trade of the metals.

Why Does This Only Apply to Americans?

The legislation specifically states that it is only for American residents. This means that if you are a resident of another country, then you will still be able to enter gold and silver leveraged trades on foreign commodities exchanges and outside of the U.S. Forex companies. The Congressional laws only apply to U.S. citizens and residents, so if you reside in another country without similar restrictions, then you will be able to get around the effects of the American Frank-Dodd Reform Act.

What Institutions and Companies are Affected?

What you will find interesting about the ruling is that it does not apply to all American companies. The rules only outlaw such margin or leveraged transactions in commodities with parties who are not either eligible commercial entities or eligible contract participants.

So if you are a commercial enterprise in a business that makes use of gold and silver and that needs to hedge against price changes in the metals, then you will still be allowed to take on gold and silver futures contracts.

Banks, hedge funds, and mutual funds will not be able to participate in this leveraged trade of gold and silver anymore. These are exactly the parties that the Frank-Dodd Reform Act is seeking to eliminate from the futures and commodities markets. The age of the American speculator is coming to an inglorious end with this act.

What Does This Mean for the Silver and Gold Prices?

The net effects of this legislation as it pertains to gold and silver are intended to stop behind the scenes speculation. One result of the Commodities and Futures Trading Commission, or CFTC, stopping this speculation trade in commodities is supposed to be more stable and transparent markets for these commodities. In theory, this will lead to more stable gold and silver prices with less violent price swings and moves on any given day.

Whether the attempt to stop the speculation trade in precious metals will work out this way in practice is debatable. The center for the world precious metals trade is London, where the London Bullion Association is based, not New York or Chicago.

There is nothing to stop speculators from trading gold and silver contracts in London, Zurich, Tokyo, Singapore, Sydney, or other foreign exchange financial centers around the world. The net result of this jurisdictional limitation may simply be that the speculation trade in silver and gold leaves the U.S. in favor of other less regulated countries.

Whatever happens with these particular issues, you can bet that more   regulations will arise as a result of the Franklin-Dodd Reform Act. The act calls for sixty-seven studies and twenty-two reports to be made on   the new regulations and oversight. Does it sound like there is any end   in sight to American regulation now that the new act is taking effect?

Investing

<u>MINDSET</u>

"Changing Habits, Attitudes and Intentions"

Seven Obsolete Concepts About Money And Getting Rich

When you went to school, you were taught a standard set of axioms for how to succeed in life and make money. These ideas were supposed to set you on your way towards prosperity and even wealth.

American society still teaches you these time worn values, such as to get a good education, to land a job that pays well, to work hard, to save as much money as you can, to invest this in mutual funds, to own your own home, and to try to be debt free.

These concepts worked well in the past industrial age, but they do not any longer in today's information age. In the following paragraphs, you will learn about these seven outdated ideas and why they are no longer relevant in your quest to grow wealthy.

1. Get a Good Education

Now, there is nothing wrong with the goal to obtain a good education. The problem with the maxim that you should get one is that the standard American education does not teach you how to manage money, finances, and investments. It instead shows you how to get a job to make ends meet and to pay your taxes. The type of education that you need to make money and work towards wealth is mostly a self taught one.

You have to read books that show you how to effectively manage your money. You must learn how to save aggressively so that you are able to invest wisely. You can learn a lot of these elusive lessons from books and articles. You may pick up others at seminars. Unfortunately, for the majority of Americans like yourself, you will not learn them in the classrooms of the American education system.

2. Find a Good Paying Job

You may shake your head when you learn that for you to seek out a high paying job is not good advice any longer. This is partly a result of the conscious devaluing of the dollar that the government has pursued aggressively since President Nixon took America off of the stable gold standard back in 1971. Once upon a time, you could count on savings and a good salary to keep up with the pace of real inflation.

Since the dollar has lost over ninety-five percent of its purchasing power since 1971 against gold, silver, oil, and other commodities, this is certainly no longer the case today. Besides the reality that the waning value of your salary is a problem, you suffer from the government's choice to aggressively penalize money that they classify as earned income.

As much as fifty percent of the money that you bring in as earned income is taken away in state and Federal income taxes. So between the outrageous penalties on earnings and the continuously lower value of your earned dollars, the idea that you can possibly earn your way to real wealth has grown less and less relevant over time.

3. Work Hard

Hard work certainly built up the United States historically. You are still taught these virtues in school. The problem with this idea is that the adage to work smarter not harder is far more appropriate under today's tax regime and declining dollar scenarios. These days, the harder that you work, the more taxes you will pay.

As if this is not punishment enough, thanks to our graduating tax system, when you work harder and make more money, you will also be forced to pay a higher tax rate too. This is the two edged sword that the government holds over the head of those who believe the idea that hard work will make them wealthy.

4. Save as Much Money as Possible

What could be wrong with the goal to save as much money as possible? When you simply save money, you probably put it into a low interest savings account. If you are more savvy than this, you might keep it in a money market account or certificate of deposit. The problem with all of these vehicles is that they are paying such a low interest rate now, you are losing real value to the constant dual ravages of inflation and the devalued dollar purchasing value.

While it is always a good idea to save money, you must quickly move it over to a sensible investment in order to keep apace of the five to ten percent loss that your purchasing power has suffered on average since 1971 because of both the devaluations and inflation. When you simply put your savings into a traditional savings vehicle, then you will actually lose ground every year.

5. Invest in Mutual Funds

Mutual funds are the darling of Wall Street, in particular for working people. The retirement specialists community has preached to you and all Americans to extol their virtues for nearly two decades now. The problem with these funds is that they only go up when the stock market gains. As you have been painfully reminded in the last few years, they can drop much faster than they go up in value.

It is very important that you instead learn to diversify your investments away from those that depend solely on the appreciation and growth of capital to do well. Real estate is a category that moves somewhat independently from the stock market.

A better way to diversify is in gold and silver. When the markets and the dollar go down in value, they go up in price. You have to learn to invest in assets that can perform well and bring gains to your portfolio regardless of how the nation's economy, banking system, and finances are doing, especially in today's day and age.

6. Own Your Home

You will be hard pressed to find a financial analyst or retirement specialist who does not tell you that you must own your home in order to be in the best possible position for retirement. This is a claim that goes unchallenged most of the time. When you stop to look at it over the long term, though, home prices have not really gone up very much, in particular as compared to some alternative investments.

In fact, when you consider the average real estate prices in the United States today versus one hundred years ago, in real dollars terms, they are about even. For most of the decades over the last hundred years, they have not gained much or at all in constant dollar value.

If you try to rely on timing the present housing market collapse bottom, you may get burned for the long term, especially if the much dreaded and apparent double dip housing recession fully materializes. This is why it can be smart to rent the place you live, or at least to use the bank's money to buy a house rather than buying it with your own. Besides that when you live in your own house you have a liability and not an asset.

7. Be Debt Free

You always hear that you should live debt free. In the information age, it is far better to learn to do like the wealthy and use other people's money to acquire assets. This is the important difference between bad debts and good debts. Bad debts are those that do not put money in your accounts but only take it away, such as purchases of cars, boats, RV's, and even houses. Good debts are the ones that permit you to acquire assets that yield passive income to create a positive cash flow and a surplus.

So now that your old misconceptions that school taught you regarding how to achieve wealth have been debunked, what will you change to take more appropriate steps towards wealth in today's circumstances?

The Solomon Secret - 7 Principles of Financial Success

There have been many financial guides and gurus for you to listen to over the years. This helps to explain why there is no shortage of wealthy people who have written books on how you can become successful and rich too.

Only one man in history can lay claim to the title of richest man ever though. This is King Solomon of Israel from the Ancient World. He is the subject of author and speaker Bruce Fleet's book "The Solomon Secret: 7 Principles of Financial Success".

In the following paragraphs you will learn why this book is an interesting read that can teach you some good lessons for success in your life, finances, and quest for wealth.

About the Author Bruce Fleet

has plenty of experience to help you manage your money. He served as the Senior Vice President of Investments for UBS in the U.S. and has been a Chairman's Council Member there as well. In this role, Bruce managed so much money for foundations around the United States that he became among the biggest advisers for charity's money in the country.

He is also the founder of a successful wealth management company Fleet Capital Management.

Even though he keeps busy with many other activities, such as speaking, writing, and even recording music, he still serves as chairman of the Fleet Capital Management group.

Besides this, Bruce is the CEO for Church Capital Finance. He has written another successful book called "Demystifying Wall Street." King Solomon is someone whom he greatly admires. This really shows in his latest book "The Solomon Secret."

Brief Background of King Solomon

Solomon proved to be the king of a united kingdom of Israel who reigned around three thousand years ago. He is called both the wisest, as well as the richest, man of all time. His exploits at trade and wealth building were so successful that they spawned legends of gold mines in Africa, stories that spread around the world, and even a few blockbuster movies.

He wrote most of a book in the Bible called Provers that deals with practical advice to help you live and take care of your personal finances. Even though his advice is almost three thousand years old, it is still relevant for you today. There are a number of people who think of King Solomon as the earliest financial writer and adviser from whom we still have his advice and work.

What is the Premise of The Solomon Secret?

Bruce Fleet starts with the idea that as the richest man who has ever lived, Solomon should have a wealth of ideas to share with and teach you. He explores the idea of what you might ask Solomon and learn from him about how to increase your wealth and live a successful life if he still lived today.

The book sets out to answer not only these questions, but also to deal with how you might apply his life example and wisdom to your own world and society. Is it really possible to transpose the ideas that Solomon discovered three thousand years ago to your modern day world of today? Bruce Fleet begins "The Solomon Secret" with the premise that you can do all of these things.

How Does The Solomon Secret Relate the Wisdom of Solomon?

Writer Bruce Fleet takes an interesting approach in his efforts to share the life, times, and wisdom of King Solomon with you. He cobbles together all of the instructional parables that Solomon offered to a man that he took on as an apprentice. This young man was named Abidan, and he became something of a protegee to King Solomon.

Abidan was actually the son to a woodworker that Solomon had pledged to instruct in the ways that you build wealth. This makes the book a more interesting read for people who are not prepared for strenuous financial advice the whole way through, as Fleet makes it a point to share with you more than just Solomon's advice.

Solomon taught seven different principals to Abidan to help him live a successful and prosperous life. These incredible lessons that Solomon relayed to his protegee are detailed in the work. Each one makes up its own interesting chapter. Before Abidan is able to achieve a greater measure of wealth and happiness, he must master each lesson.

Solomon teaches principals on diversification, long term planning, how to have business savvy, and ethical business dealings.

At the conclusion of each chapter, Fleet shows you how the teaching from Solomon pertains to the world and your life today. The mix between life stories and powerful lessons that deal with finance, work, and life are all relayed by the author in such a way that you can apply them to your own life.

Does the Advice from the Solomon Secret Work?

The lessons that are taught from King Solomon are well accepted today. They have been used and re-taught in the thousands of years since Solomon's time on the earth ended. If you are wondering how this advice can still be relevant to you today, the answer is simple.

They are applicable to you because these are not simply lessons on how to build wealth. They are financial laws on the means that you can use to create wealth for yourself and your family. Natural laws of the universe are timeless. This is the reason that they worked so well thousands of years ago and will still work in centuries to come.

What is the Final Verdict of the Solomon Secret?

The book is really two stories in one. There is the story of the author and his own real life financial mistakes that he made along his journey. This provides a level of honesty that you do not always see from financial writers. It also provides a personal connection that helps to draw readers in who can relate to people that live in today's world.

Beyond this, "The Solomon Secret" focuses on the life and lessons of King Solomon.

The beauty of the work is the way that author Bruce Fleet manages to bring these to life and make them relevant for you today. Fleet takes the parables that Solomon teaches to Abidan and incorporates a masterful application of the wisdom for your life.

He also uses the knowledge and applies it directly to the burning and critical financial queries that the country struggles with today. In this way, Fleet provides you with the most time tested and successful financial ideas that you can use to handle your own personal finances in the difficult economic environment that you live in nowadays. The end result is an enjoyable and powerful combination of financial truths and stories that teach you the means to grow both rich and wise.

You have no shortage of financial gurus to choose from anymore. There are so many books on personal finance that are full of advice for how you can achieve wealth out there today. Given the choice, would you rather read a dry, boring book on finance, or one filled with personal stories, insight, and application offered from a legendary and wealthy ancient king who still fires the imagination of people today?

Achieve Financial Freedom Through The Power of Education

If you are like most Americans, then you would like to learn the ways to get ahead and to secure your financial freedom. The main obstacle that stands in your way is actually simple. You do not know how to gain financial freedom.

It may surprise you to learn that the methods for you to reach these goals do not revolve around hard work, a savings account, or a good 401 k retirement plan. For you to achieve your dreams of financial independence, you must start with the power of education.

The subsequent paragraphs will show you how you should proceed in your quest for a good financial education that you lack along with the majority of Americans.

The Reason You Are Not Taught About Finances in School

There is a reason that you do not learn about financial education in school. The present day school model was not designed to create investors or business leaders. The founders of the public school system philosophy set it up to teach the masses how to be good employees.

In the early nineteen hundreds, when the states were just beginning to make schooling compulsory, John D. Rockefeller and Frederick Gates created a philanthropic trust called the General Education Board. With its initial start up grant of a hundred and eighty million dollars, this group had enormous influence on the philosophy and spread of public education throughout America.

The goals that they successfully promoted in education were demonstrated in their 1906 statement. The General Education Board did not seek to create investors, business men, philosophers, or scientists. It stated a goal to organize children to learn to do the same jobs that their parents did in a more effective manner.

Public education became a means to train children up to be employees like their parents. There was no impetus to provide financial education at all.

The most important thing for you to take away from this public school history is that it is not your fault that you did not learn about finances and how to manage your money to achieve financial freedom in school. The state and Federal governments did not set up the system to accomplish this. What matters now is that you take the control of your personal financial education into your own hands.

Don't Follow Wall Street or the Government for Your Financial Advice

You may be saying that you do not have to worry about your future finances at all, since you have the brokers on Wall Street and the government to help advise you for your financial future.

These are both dangerous sources to seek help from if you wish to achieve true financial freedom.

Wall Street, its firms, and their employees have one overarching goal in mind. This is to make as much money for themselves as they possibly can. In order to do this, they need you to simply put your savings into mutual funds on a regular basis so that you will support the stock prices and help them to gradually keep rising.

Along the way, they will be happy to advise you in this course of action in exchange for hefty fees that amount to as much as three hundred thousand dollars over a thirty year period. Ultimately, they will do what is best for them. Your financial independence is not a part of their short term or long term goals.

If you think that the government will take care of you instead, then you had best think again. The government's finances are on increasingly shaky ground. The long term outlook for the U.S. debt and financial picture has been cut in mid April to negative by S&P Ratings agency. It is highly possible that the government's credit rating will be lowered.

Whether they suffer from this eventual fate or not, even the negative outlook will make it more difficult for them to continue to finance future obligations like social security. Certainly retirement benefits will have to be reduced and the minimum retirement age increased before long.

When you trust in them to provide for your financial future, you are not taking a proactive stance to improve your situation. You are only taking a calculated risk that the government will be able to provide for you in a meaningful way.

Where Can You Obtain Good Financial Education?

There are a number of places where you can obtain good financial education. Usually you will need to get some books and articles on finance and investments to begin. There are so many of these on the market today. Robert Kiyosaki's Rich Dad series is a good place to start. You should also train yourself to routinely read a good financial publication, like The Wall Street Journal, Forbes, or Baron's. All of these are available online nowadays.

You can also enroll in special classes that your area college or community college offers. They will have classes on how to manage your money and investments for yourself. Seminars on the subject are another good choice. Practically every large metropolitan area in the country sees seminars come through the area that include such topics as how you can invest in real estate or stocks.

You can also find many more seminars online that cover advanced financial education themes like ways to generate passive income. You should invest the time, effort, and cost in some of these to start building your financial knowledge up now.

What Should You Do While You Are Educating Yourself?

You need to be as proactive as possible with your personal finances. It is critical for you to begin to set financial goals. If you do not have financial goals that you are actively working towards, then you can count on being at roughly the same place in five years where you are today. These will vary from one individual to another, but will have several characteristics in common.

Among the first of your goals should be to start to pay yourself before you pay your bills and expenses.

You can have your employer take ten percent of your paycheck and direct deposit it into a separate account. You should make it a goal to save money that you proactively invest so that you can generate inbound cash flow.

In the beginning, you will have to change your whole mindset about money. It is all too easy to see money as something that you spend as soon as it comes in, or that you save in a low interest savings account. Instead of you looking at money as something that you never have enough of or that only grows slowly in savings accounts, you have to begin to see it as a tool that you can put to work for yourself.

Money is a means that allows you to acquire assets that produce income. For you to become a financially independent person does not mean that you have millions of dollars in the bank. Instead, your mindset about financial freedom should be to have enough money that comes in every month so that you can reach the point where your money works hard enough for you so that you do not have to work a job. Is that not what financial freedom is about ultimately?

Financial Planning - A Key Ingredient For Building Wealth

Financial planning is a term that you have probably heard before. Yet despite the fact that you may know the phrase, it is very possible that you are not familiar with what the term financial planning precisely means.

Financial planning is a concept that you must understand and implement in your personal finances. Thanks to the recent financial crisis that has impacted investment accounts and upset so many people's retirement plans around the world, it is more important now than ever before.

In the paragraphs below, you will learn all about financial planning and how it is the key in your efforts to build up wealth.

What Does Financial Planning Entail?

To understand what financial planning entails, you should first comprehend what it means. Financial planning refers to the procedure where you set up goals; decide what resources, income, and assets you have; think about your financial needs and dreams for the future; and then set plans and take concrete steps towards your reaching those end goals.

Financial planning is often misunderstood to be all about retirement, but it is useful in your quest to achieve any kind of financial goals. Besides working towards retirement, these goals could also be to pay for a child's college education, to leave money to you family, or to reach the point of financial independence where you do not have to work to support yourself well in advance of retirement years. You will find many different components comprise this financial planning. These include allocating your assets, pursuing investments, and managing your risk.

When you allocate your assets, you are simply diversifying, or dividing your money into different types of investments. This means that you do not put all of your hard earned money into just stocks, bonds, or mutual funds. These tend to go up and down together, as they are all correlated to how well the overall economy performs. You manage your risk when you spread your investment dollars around to different types and classes of assets, or holdings.

Why Should You Practice Financial Planning?

In today's economy, the reasons that you should practice financial planning are more apparent. Through this type of financial planning, you are able to stretch your dollars to the maximum potential. When you do it practically and consistently, it will allow you to determine what your priorities are financially and to steadfastly move towards these medium to longer range goals.

Financial planning will also allow you to build up reserves against an emergency or unforeseen disaster. How long could you survive if you lost your job, had your salary significantly cut back, or became too ill to work? What if you need to or want to change jobs into an area that will provide a better income for you and your family or more satisfaction for your career?

These are very legitimate concerns in the real world today that financial planning can help you to address in your own life. Financial planning will enable you to create an emergency fund and additional streams of income that can help to support you should any of these events occur. It will also help you to feel more confident and in control of your daily life. All of this also permits you to sleep better, and you know how valuable a good night's sleep can be.

Why Has Financial Planning Become More Important For You Than Ever?

Financial planning is more necessary now than at any point since the Great Depression. This is partly because unemployment is so high and jobs are still very difficult to find and secure. You can no longer count on easy credit terms from credit cards and loans as you could in the past boom years. These days, you must have financial reserves ready not only for emergencies, but also for future goals and dreams.

Is it Necessary to Hire a Professional Financial Planner?

A number of people choose to engage the services of a professional financial planner. This is because they are knowledgeable on a number of different topics that are related to such planning. Some of them are certified financial planners. All of them will have some amount of experience to bring to your particular situation.

They can be especially helpful for you who have a greater amount of assets and income sources. Financial planners must be paid though. Another thing to remember is that ultimately no one has your own best interests at heart more than you do.

If you choose to do your own financial planning, you are not all alone in the task. You can buy a financial planning computer program. There are also numerous good books on the subject available from your area bookstore or local library. You can even download financial planning guides off of the Internet these days.

There are so many resources that you can use for this activity online. So long as you are willing to invest the time and research that is necessary in order to do the project, you can successfully complete your own financial planning.

What Are Some Practical Tips for Financial Planning?

Financial planning starts with you making a goal to save money. This will require more than just to hope for it to happen. You must pay yourself first before you pay your bills and other expenses. Many employers will be able to take part of your pay check out and direct deposit it into a separate account. This way, you will not even miss the money or struggle to put it to the side every month.

Another key in your financial planning is to invest the money and diversify it. Do not simply leave it to languish in a savings account that pays near zero percent interest. Instead, put it to work in investments that produce income streams. Your strategy will not be the same as every other person's plan.

You might consider high yield dividend stocks, real estate investment trusts, or oil and gas trusts. All of these will provide you with a nice extra source of income when you build up your holdings. They have the added advantage of being very liquid, or easy to buy and sell.

You should also put at least a portion of your saved money into investments that are not correlated to each other.

This means that you should look into investments that are not all dollar denominated. You might struggle to think of investments that are not priced in only dollars, but there are some very good choices available to you in the precious metals such as gold and silver.

What Are Some Examples and Consequences of Financial Planning?

There are three different groups of people who plan for different time horizons with predictable results. Those who plan their finances for the next weekend are the poor. Those individuals who make their plan for a retirement horizon turn out to be the middle class.

Finally, the people who craft financial plans for generations are the rich. It should not come as any surprise to you that those who plan for tomorrow have nothing while those who think ahead for the distant future are the wealthy.

Which of the three types of financial planners are you?

Share Your Advice - Get Inside The Expert Industry

If you have ever thought that you would like to start a career as a self help guru or expert, then you have probably talked yourself out of it as too difficult and mysterious a task for you to seriously begin. This has certainly been the case for most people in the past, since there was no manual on how to begin such an enterprise.

From an outsider's point of view, the speaker circuit seems like it is crowded enough already, and yet another self help success appears all the time. The mystique that surrounds this industry has finally been lifted for you.

In the paragraphs that follow, you will see why the book "The Millionaire Messenger: Make a Difference and a Fortune Sharing Your Advice" by Brendon Burchard is exactly the instructional guide that you need in order to approach this exciting and rewarding opportunity for your future.

About the Author Brendon Burchard

It makes sense that the writer of a guide that teaches you to launch a self help guru career would have a vast amount of experience in the business himself to share with you. Brendon Burchard is ideally suited to this role. The author has proven his career as a self help expert and made multiple millions at it.

Besides this, Burchard has founded the Experts Academy, the place that provides the most all inclusive training in the world for people who are or who want to become experts on advice. He makes appearances, authors newsletters and books, and produces products that motivate more than two million individuals every year. Among his past successes is the book "Life's Golden Ticket." Burchard today remains among the most successful and well known motivational speakers and business trainers on earth.

Get Inside The Expert Industry

You will not find much disagreement on the observation that the industry of experts is one that is little understood and even secretive. Brendon Burchard set out to change this image and reality with "The Millionaire Messenger."

In the work, he explains to you that he was fortunate enough to be given life's golden ticket of a second chance when he survived the ordeal of a terrible car accident. Since then, he has made it his life's work to help you and other people find your true voice so that you can live your life to the fullest and chase your dreams.

Brendon Burchard does this so that you can learn to become a well known and well paid expert on advice. The goal is to show you how to make a living doing this when you give speeches or seminars, coach others, consult for companies and organizations, and author books, websites, and programs online. This does not sound like an easy undertaking, yet it is the goal that the author has set out with the book. It is why Brendon Burchard has earned the nickname the guru of the gurus.

The Millionaire Messenger Teaches You to Become A Successful Expert

The author Brendon Burchard is well acquainted with the mass appeal and popular acceptance of ten step programs. He sets one out in the book to show you exactly how you can become a successful and sought out expert.

When you use this ten step program of his that he calls "ten steps to an expert empire," then you will be able to package up your successes, struggles, life stories, or even research into marketable advice that will make you into an successful expert on a topic.

Along with a ten step advice program on how to become a successful advice guru professional, Burchard has many important lessons to teach you on the practical things that you need to know to become this self help expert. You will learn that the story of your own life and experiences contains tremendous lessons. These are likely more significant and valuable than you ever before contemplated.

Even so, it is not enough to know that your real life experience has potential great value to other people. You have to learn another "Millionaire Messenger" lesson. This is that your purpose on earth is to make a real difference to other people and the world.

The most effective way to accomplish this is to gather and compile all of your own outlook, knowledge, expertise, and voice on a given topic that will motivate other individuals to reach their true potential.

Knowledge and calling are two of the necessary mindsets for you to become a self help expert. The third one is the realization that you can earn money when you share your knowledge, perspective, and advice with people. As you do this, you can watch your efforts grow into an extremely profitable business that will also give you a deep and rich satisfaction in your own life.

The Difference Between You and Successful Experts You See on TV

"The Millionaire Messenger" addresses the question about what separates the experts that you watch on TV from you and everyone else. These gurus who are everywhere online, in books, at seminars, and on the television are not so much amazing individuals that you can never aspire to be like.

In fact, they are mostly regular and even ordinary people that have taken their successes and struggles in life, or their life story, or even research that they have done and bundled it up into a neat, understandable, and appealing package.

It is not so important what their subject of expertise is. They might teach you how to open a business, live passionately, succeed in work, or raise a happier family. What they have done that you have not is to realize that their own experiences and lessons are their greatest assets and legacies in life. They understand that you can be paid when you bring your message of hope or accomplishment out to the world.

Choose Your Topic To Become An Expert

The best thing about Brendon Burchard's ten step program on how you become an expert has to do with subject matter.

You might be worried that your particular experiences will not fit the proper mold of self help.

You are not limited to any one topic or even type of topic when you use his method to success. With his chapters titled, "The Millionaire Messenger's Money Map," "Behind the Guru Curtain," and "The Millionaire Mandates," he shows you how any type of self help category can make you a success.

A Must Read Story How Self Help Gurus Succeed

Maybe you have always wanted to be a self help guru or followed expert yourself. The idea that you can serve other people and create a lucrative business along the way appeals to you. Maybe you do not personally aspire to this, but you are still interested to learn how the gurus actually accomplish it.

In either case, "The Millionaire Mindset" will thrill and inspire you with the real life tale of how Brendon Burchard became among the best regarded and most successful self help motivational speakers and authors in the world. This is the must read story of how self help gurus succeed in their missions. What will you learn from this exciting industry?

The Five Unfair Advantages To Master The Financial Crisis

Since he burst onto the scene with his hugely successful book "Rich Dad, Poor Dad," Robert Kiyosaki has become a mainstay in the personal finance self help category. This success is not undeserved, since his "Rich Dad, Poor Dad" book remains the top selling personal financial book ever.

Robert has turned his original mega best seller into an entire brand under the Rich Dad company name. Robert Kiyosaki's latest foray under the brand is the book "Unfair Advantage: The Power of Financial Education."

This book goes a step further than his earlier works, since it is updated to give an explanation for who caused the financial meltdown and economic crisis that began in 2007.

About the Author Robert Kiyosaki

Robert Kiyosaki has a wide variety of experiences that he brings to the financial self help industry. He started out as a businessman and became an investor before he began his self help author and motivational speaker career. Since the Rich Dad brand exploded with his first success "Rich Dad, Poor, Dad," Robert has penned fifteen books that together boast in excess of twenty-six million copies sold.

Three of these works have actually been listed on top ten best selling lists of The New York Times, USA Today, and The Wall Street Journal at the same time. Besides writing books and speaking, author Kiyosaki has developed three "Cashflow" software and board games for children and adults.

He also puts out a series of disks on the Rich Dad concept. Robert certainly deserve your attention as he helped tens of millions of individuals throughout the globe change the ways that they understand and relate to money.

What is the Premise of Unfair Advantage?

Robert's latest book "Unfair Advantage - The Power of Financial Education" does more than simply offer you a series of unfair advantages that you can have for yourself. It explains the ways that the wealthy become wealthier even when a financial crisis takes place.

It also goes into detail on who is to blame for the financial collapse. Kiyosaki takes a hard look at the problems that the country still faces. He goes behind the curtain to show you who caused the sub prime mortgage meltdown. In hard hitting style, he names the names of the guilty parties.

Beyond this illumination, "Unfair Advantage" shows you actual solutions that you can put to work for yourself to resolve real problems. You should not look at this as your one stop get rick quick manual. Instead, you should use it as a spotlight to show you the areas where your financial education is not yet where it needs to be so that you can take proactive steps towards wealth.

Kiyosaki also makes it a point with "Unfair Advantage" to show you the various financial struggles that other people deal with today. Your financial world faces challenges like you probably have not encountered before in your lifetime. Robert Kiyosaki demonstrates that people of all backgrounds and places in life struggle with disadvantages and obstacles.

He tells you to change your whole mindset about these challenges. You can not simply believe that you are financially disadvantaged and settle on the idea that you have very few choices and options. Kiyosaki correctly points out that if you do, you will struggle with money and finances for your entire life. "Unfair Advantage" makes it a point to give you real steps that you can take action on to improve your situation.

Naturally, this begins with education that you can apply to your own situation to get real results that you can see and measure. This financial education is your real unfair advantage, and Kiyosaki goes through five areas that you must learn about in order to succeed.

Unfair Advantage 1: Knowledge

The first unfair advantage that you must start with is knowledge. This encompasses many things, from knowledge about how to handle your finances sensibly to knowledge about the right kinds of investments.

The old adage that knowledge is power is a cornerstone of the unfair advantages that you will learn in the book.

Unfair Advantage 2: Taxes

The next unfair advantage that you have to internalize pertains to the tax system. The tax system does not treat all types of income equally at all. It penalizes workers and their earned income with high tax rates of up to thirty-five percent. At the same time, it gives advantages to investors, who typically pay no more than fifteen percent in long term capital gains and taxes on dividends.

You can even make money that is basically not taxed when you invest in properties and ventures that produce oil and gas or in some forms of real estate that provide housing for people or office spaces for businesses.

Unfair Advantage 3: Debt

A third unfair advantage that the book discusses is debt. Kiyosaki is quick to distinguish between bad and good debt. Bad debts are those that take money out of your pocket and do not provide an income stream. This includes credit cards, large mortgages, and other similar debts.

Good debts are those that give you an income stream that pays the costs associated with the debt and also provide you with cash flow and additional income. Rental properties are an example of this type of good debt. When you learn how to properly use other people's money to leverage good debt for smart investments, you will have a tremendous unfair advantage over others who do not do this.

Unfair Advantage 4: Risk

Another unfair advantage revolves around ways to handle and manage risk. Risk is not something of which you have to be afraid. It is something that you can use to gain larger returns on your investments. You must know how to manage it successfully.

Unfair Advantage 5: Compensation

A last unfair advantage that this book will teach you about involves compensation. You will always have advantages when you run a business for yourself instead of work to make someone else wealthy. Practically no one gets rich when he or she works for someone else. The best and most rewarding compensation is the one that you make when you work on your own behalf. Kiyosaki shows you how to do this.

Final Verdict on Unfair Advantage

"Unfair Advantage - The Power of Financial Education" could possibly be the most helpful book that Robert Kiyosaki has written yet. Some of his other books have been accused of being reworkings of his earlier triumphs.

This is certainly not the case with "Unfair Advantage." Kiyosaki does bring in some material from his earlier works, but he also provides you with a great amount of new and fresh information, along with actions that you can take to better your own financial education and then put it to practical use for yourself.

Kiyosaki is famous for answering the question "what would you do with ten thousand dollars" with the response that you should invest it in your own financial education so that you can answer the question for yourself. Start with this book, and you will understand the things that you must learn in order to manage your own money and investments.

How will you better your financial education today?

Liabilities Take More Money Away From You Than You Think

When you prepare to make a significant purchase of a consumer item, you probably do not think of this boat, car, television, or stereo equipment as a liability. It is easy to confuse assets and liabilities, but the two are actually the opposite of one another.

Any item that you purchase will fall under one of the two categories. The fact is that the goods that you purchase have an opportunity cost beyond the literal expense of the item itself. In the paragraphs that follow, you will learn what the difference is between an asset and a liability and what the real cost of a purchase may actually be to you over time.

What Does the Term Assets Mean?

Assets are often considered to be any item that you own that possesses value. A true asset though is one that brings in money to you on a consistent basis. Such earning assets create revenue streams for you simply because you own them. More than just a representation of value, a real asset is one that will make money for you. These assets bring in money without requiring that you work to earn the money. Retirement plans and investments are both assets.

They contribute a steady stream of income that you can use to to cover your costs in retirement or to increase your cash flow.

There are many different types of assets that you might have, like money market accounts, stocks, bonds, rental real estate, e-commerce web sites, royalties on creative works, or patents on inventions.

Once you have paid for these assets, they start to bring money back to you almost immediately in the form of a consistent income stream. You can also sell your assets and receive a lump sum for them at most any time. Once you do this, they will not provide you with consistent periodic income any longer.

What Does the Term Liabilities Mean?

Liabilities have several meanings. They represent obligations that you have. A debt that you have not paid is always a liability, even if you own something against it like a house or a car. Liabilities can be short term or long term.

Debts that you will pay off in under a year are considered to be short term. Debts that you will pay for a time frame of over a year, such as a car payment or mortgage, are long term liabilities. There are many examples of liabilities in debts that you owe. Lines of credit, mortgages, second mortgages, car payments, and liens of all types are each liabilities.

A liability is also any item that costs you money, or takes money away from you. This means that a house that you owe money on is a liability and not an asset. A boat that you make payments on falls under the category of liability as well. Even a boat that you have paid for is a liability as it will cost you significant money every month in maintenance, upkeep, and dock fees.

The definition of liability can also extend to things that you buy that only cost you money upfront. Even though a flat screen television may not cost you money every month to own, it presents an opportunity cost. This is because the resources that you commit to purchase this consumer good are lost to you.

With the money that you spend on the television, you might have instead choose to purchase an investment that brings in money to you on a regular basis, such as a stock that pays dividends, corporate bonds that pay interest, or real estate or oil and gas trusts that pay out shares of the rents and resource sales.

All of these investments that provide you with routine income would count as assets. The flat screen television that takes money away from you to purchase it and does not bring any money back in to you over time is a liability.

Liabilities Distract You From Creating Assets

Liabilities do more than simply take money away from you. They also distract you and keep you from a focus on ways to create assets that bring you in money. When you have to think about how you will pay your mortgage payment, car payment, and other bills, it saps your energy and breaks your concentration.

In the example of the flat screen television, the consumer good can very literally take your focus away from the development of assets. Few things can cause a greater distraction than endless hours spent in front of the TV. Your lost time that you could instead spend starting an e-commerce site, developing a side business, or learning how to invest is invaluable and can never be replaced.

This is a definition of liabilities that you probably have never before considered. Yet lost time very much describes resources that go out every month. If time is money, then distractions cost you plenty and represent considerable liabilities.

The Real Cost of Such Liabilities

You may still be struggling with the concept of how the flat screen television is a liability. How come it costs you more to own it than the one thousand dollars with which you buy it? This is where the concept of opportunity cost comes in to play. Opportunity costs refers to other options that you had for the money that you spend on the flat screen TV.

Assume that you purchase this television for the one thousand dollars. Keep in mind that you might have instead put this money into some investments that generate income. If you invest the thousand dollars into a high yield investment that pays fifteen percent each year, then you will receive one hundred and fifty dollars each year in additional income.

That may not sound like so much at first, but think about these returns over five years. Now you are talking about one hundred and fifty dollars times five, or seven hundred and fifty dollars. Your original thousand dollars would now be worth seventeen hundred and fifty dollars.

Over ten years, it would amount to fifteen hundred dollars that would bring your total amount from one thousand dollars to twenty-five hundred dollars. Given twenty years time, the return would be three thousand dollars, and this would increase your total from the one thousand dollars to four thousand dollars.

None of these examples assume that you reinvest the gains each year either. For example, the second year you could reinvest your one hundred and fifty dollar gains from the first year and have eleven hundred and fifty dollars to earn returns on the next year. This way, at the end of the second year you would have thirteen hundred and twenty-two dollars.

By the end of five years, this would bring you up to two thousand eleven dollars. Over ten or twenty years time, it would amount to even larger amounts. At the end of ten years, you would have four thousand and forty-five dollars.

By the time you reached twenty years, your total investment would grow through constantly reinvesting the returns to over eight thousand dollars. How much does that appealing thousand dollar television really cost you to buy in lost opportunity cost?

<u>ECONOMY</u>

"Managing Resources for Prosperity"

Inflation Top Financial Trend in 2011 - What Can You Do?

By now, you have probably heard the warning alarm that many reputable and respected people are sounding about inflation that will come in the future.

The number of economists, financial writers, and investors that have raised the specter of imminent inflation grows every week.

A well respected financial magazine has just joined the chorus on inflation concerns. This is Money Magazine that highlights inflation as the top trend in 2011. Inflation is not just a scary sounding financial word that only economists and government policy makers like the Federal Reserve have to worry about.

Since it is possible that it will be the top trend in 2011, inflation is something that you need to understand and plan for to protect your money and investments this year. The following paragraphs explain why inflation is such a threat now and what you can do about it before it arrives.

What Exactly Is Inflation?

There are a number of definitions for inflation. It is the continuous increase in the average level of costs of goods and services. When you see inflation in the economy, the general prices are going up. It signifies that your money is declining in purchasing power.

Inflation is commonly counted as a yearly percentage increase. Inflation is also an event that is driven by money. The all too common phrase inflation is too many dollars that are after too few goods captures the concept well.

Inflation is created in the United States when the government decides to alter the amount of money that circulates in the economy and financial system. As the government makes the decision to print too much money, then dollars become too readily available as compared to the relatively constant amount of goods and services that businesses offer.

> *Inflation is therefore directly produced as the quantity of dollars goes up more than the amounts of goods and services that are made available.*

If you have not paid attention to financial television or various financial publications, then you may have missed the ominous tally that shows that the Federal government has boosted the amount of dollars in circulation in the country and the world by in excess of three hundred percent since the housing collapse, financial crisis, and Great Recession began in 2007.

So far, you have not seen any inflation to speak of as a result of this shocking and massive increase in the money supply. That will most likely change this year.

The Inflation Wave Is Coming

It is Money Magazine that has brought to the forefront what so many wealthy and knowledgeable investors have said for more than a year or two now. In their most current issue, Money

Magazine has warned you that the major new trend for 2011 is that the Federal Reserve is going to reinflate the national economy.

 This will create substantial inflation as a result.

The issue is called the Investor Guide for 2011. Money magazine goes through a number of different ideas and suggestions in the issue. Out of all of them, inflation is described as the biggest trend that you need to be looking out for this year.

The Equity Research Director Pat Dorsey of Morningstar, one of the most successful and respected advisory and ranking service publications, is quoted a lot in the article about inflation. He says that after he heard and studied the various recent statements that the Fed has made, he is sure that the country's central banking committee will choose to reinflate the American economy by using any and all means at their disposal.

He goes on to point out that it is not easy to properly reinflate an economy in such a way that jobs are created and yet inflation does not rise substantially as a result. Dorsey says that no such examples of this successful and exact macroeconomic level of adjustments are offered by history. This is his main reason for arguing that the Federal Reserve with the very best of intentions will overdo it. Remember all of the massive boost in the money supply that is lurking in the shadows and waiting to drive the prices up as well.

Other Financial People Who Warn About Inflation

The legendary billionaire investor Warren Buffet, who has been called America's most successful investor of all time, agrees with Money Magazine and the Morningstar equity research director.

At the shareholder meeting of his Berkshire Hathaway company this past year he claimed that the prospects of you seeing substantial amounts of inflation have gone up.

More recently, Buffet added that this nation has constantly grown its debt levels when compared to the Gross Domestic Product, or total of all goods and services produced. They have come up with this money from overseas. Eventually, you will see them inflate away the crushing burden of the debt.

Other prominent thinkers and writers who have lent their voices in support of inflation in the near future include Richard Rahn, who is chairman of the Institute for Global Economic Growth. Robert Wiedemer, the economist and co-writer of the bestselling book "Aftershock" who forecast the financial fallout more than a year before it happened, is another person predicting inflation.

Author David Skarica, who wrote the recent best seller "The Great Super Cycle, Profit from the Coming Inflation and Dollar Devaluation," believes that central banks like the Federal Reserve are already purposefully inflating the value of their nations' currencies to help make their crushing debt burdens more manageable. Skarica claims that this will cause not only inflation, but a dollar devaluation of as high as fifty percent in the next several years.

What Can You Do to Protect Your Money and Investments from Inflation This Year?

Simply selling your holdings to hoard your money in cash will not protect it.

If money is going to lose value, then one of the worst things that you can do is put it in an interest bearing money market account or CD that will not hope to keep up with the new inflation levels. There are various investments that you might place your money in to protect it from inflation.

People who hope to find stocks that will still do well in an inflationary environment might try to put some of their money in those that are inherently resistant to inflation. Real Estate Investment Trusts put your money into real estate properties and rentals.

HCN is a health care Real Estate Investment Trust that manages buildings including medical offices and senior living centers. They have protection from inflation built in to their contracts as their leases include inflation adjusters that are set to the official measurement of inflation in America, the Consumer Price Index.

Bonds typically do not well in an inflationary environment. If you had to hold on to some type of them, TIPS would probably be your best possibility. These Treasury Inflation Protected Securities offer you inflation protection, since the principal value goes up with inflation as measured by the Consumer Price Index. The interest payments that they make twice a year also go up with inflation.

The best hedge against inflation has always been precious metals, in particular gold and silver. Gold especially has been used to safeguard against currency devaluation and unstable economic times for thousands of years. You can buy both of them in physical coins and bars, or as a stock with one of the gold or silver ETF's like GLD or SLV.

What will you do to protect yourself from the strong possibility of inflation in 2011?

How Are Interest Rates And Economic Inflation Related?

You hear a lot of talk these days about how inflation has reared its ugly head once again. Even though the official government CPI, or Consumer Price Index, inflation numbers may not show the real world inflation that is rippling through the economy now, you feel it whenever you buy gas, groceries, or clothes.

What you may not understand is that a great deal of the inflation problem turns out to be caused by the prolonged period of low interest rates that you have seen since before 2008. Though the Federal Reserve has raised interest rates in order to fight inflation in the past, the real danger today is that they will not raise the interest rates much at all to fight inflation.

In the subsequent paragraphs, you will see how interest rates and inflation are interrelated and how this affects you on a personal level.

How Interest Rates Affect Healthy Economies

Healthy economies can handle fluctuations in interest rates. Lower interest rates tend to encourage individuals to borrow money with which to pursue large purchases like cars, boats, and houses.

These lower interest rates boost consumer spending directly. They also boost it indirectly, as consumers who pay lower interest rates on their loans and credit card bills have additional money to spend. Since consumer spending represents around two thirds of U.S. economic activity, you can see how important this level of spending is for the overall economy.

But the benefit from lower interest rates does not stop with you the consumer. Farmers and businesses also see advantages in lower interest rates. Since the cost to borrow money is lower, this motivates both groups to go through with big equipment purchases and other capital improvements. The final result is higher farm output and business productivity, both of which encourage the economy to grow.

As more money is created and made available to consumers, farmers, and businesses, invariably inflation appears. Too much money that chases too few goods causes prices to rise. In a healthy economy, the U.S. Federal Reserve will simply raise interest rates to reduce the amount of money that moves through the economy and fight off this inflation.

Higher interest rates translate to cut backs in the amount of money that consumer and businesses spend. Less money is available to chase the number of goods and services in the economy. This is good in the battle against inflation, but it does cause a slow down in the economy. As consumers pay larger amounts in interest, they have less disposable income. This forces them to reduce the amount of money that they spend.

Banks make a smaller number of loans to consumers. Businesses and farmers also take out fewer loans as they are not willing to spend more money on plants and equipment when consumers spend less money on goods and food. Productivity slows and businesses lay off more employees. Inflation has been reduced inversely to the higher interest rates. Your dollars' purchasing power is protected this way, but at a price.

How Interest Rates Affect Weaker Economies

When the economy is already weaker, the decision by the Fed to raise interest rates become more problematic. Higher interest rates will lower inflation as they choke off the amount of money that flows through the economy. At the same time, when the economy is weak, consumers and businesses cut back significantly on the amount of money that they spend.

Businesses may then drastically reduce payrolls. In the end, these higher interest rates often lead a weak economy into recession. Recessions happen when the economic output of the national economy declines for at least two consecutive quarters.

Recessions can become severe and last for many quarters, as in the Great Recession of 2007 to 2009. Below, you will see two examples of how the Fed has used higher interest rates to fight off inflation or lower interest rates to spur the economy into renewed economic growth.

Why Did Fed Chairman Paul Volcker Raise Interest Rates to Over 18% in the early 1980's?

In 1981, inflation had run out of control. It stood at fourteen percent a year. Paul Volcker was the chairman of the Federal Reserve at the time. He knew that drastic increases to the interest rate were necessary to bring inflation back down to a normal level.

The chairman raised interest rates to higher than 18% in his efforts to save the U.S. economy from what could be called a mild hyperinflation. It did stop and eliminate the inflation that plagued the country. Unfortunately, it also caused a severe recession.

Why Did the Fed Lower Interest Rates to 1.25% in 2001 to 2002?

On the other hand, interest rates that decline typically bring an end to recessions. The beginning of this century saw the economy devastated by the technology stocks and dot com crash. In 2001 and 2002, the Federal Reserve reduced the interest rate to 1.25%.

As the Federal Reserve lowered the rate that it charges banks, the cost to borrow money dropped along with it. People began to spend money once more and businesses hired more employees and purchased additional equipment. There can be no doubt that the significant economic rebound in 2003 resulted in large part from the interest rates that had been cut.

How Is The Fed Handling the Aftermath of the Great Recession Today?

During the Great Recession that started in 2007 and 2008, the Federal Reserve aggressively cut the interest rates down to about zero percent.

Due to a combination of extremely low interest rates and cheap money that the Fed printed, the economy has been pulled back from the brink of collapse brought on by the financial crisis.

With all of the money that the Fed and Treasury injected into the economy during the last few years, they managed to more than triple the existing supply of U.S. dollars. Inflation has begun to show up in the prices of a broad range of commodities and goods, ranging from oil, gold, silver, and copper to cotton, wheat, and corn.

This is the point where the Fed needs to show discipline and raise interest rates to prevent runaway inflation. The problem is that today there are serious obstacles that discourage the Fed from raising interest rates. In fact, it is unlikely that interest rates will be raised at all any time soon, even when inflation grows into a more serious threat.

Why Is It Unlikely that the Fed Will Raise Interest Rates?

As the Fed constantly points out, the economic recovery is still incredibly fragile. The housing market has not recovered at all. The Case Shiller Home Prices index released on April 26th showed that housing prices are once again at the low of the Great Recession.

Unemployment is still at a shockingly high almost nine percent. Besides this, the bad loans and mortgages that led to the crisis in the first place have not been addressed.

Perhaps more critically, since the crisis began, the government has increased the Federal Debt to a shocking over fourteen trillion dollars.

If the Fed raises the interest rates, they threaten to derail not only the weak economy, but also the government's ability to finance itself.

This is because higher interest rates will also mean significantly larger interest rate payments will be required of the Treasury to finance the astronomical U.S. debt. The government is already borrowing almost half of what it spends now.

Do you see them raising interest rates and increasing their interest payments any time soon?

China Will Dominate The New World Order Before 2016

You probably did not see a little known announcement that appeared on the website of the International Monetary Fund in April. Articles have since been written about it which reveal their prediction that China will surpass the United States as the largest economy in the world in 2016.

This may not at first sound like shocking news to you, but the event had not been expected to take place for at least another decade beyond this. When China passes the U.S. as global economic leader, it will mark the end of the American century.

You will likely begin to see significant and terrible ramifications for the United States as the dominant lone super power as well as for the U.S. dollar as the reserve currency of the world. In the following paragraphs, you will read about how this has happened so fast and what the consequences may be for the U.S. in the near future.

How Will China Surpass the U.S. as Largest Economy in Only Five Years?

You should understand how it is possible for China to pass the United States as the largest economy so quickly. The International Monetary Fund came up with these calculations using a different method than other forecasters have relied on in the past.

They did not compare the two nations' gross domestic products, or totals of all goods and services produced in the nations, with their currencies as the basis. Instead, they relied on purchasing power parity that measures what currencies will actually buy in the two nations.

This alternative measurement is said by many economists to be a more accurate representation of GDP, since the Chinese manipulate their currency to keep it artificially low. Currencies can also change value with astonishing speed.

When the IMF uses the purchasing power parity comparison, the Chinese economy stands at about 14% of the global total now. In five years, they project that the Chinese economy will represent more than 18% of the global whole. This would have their GDP expand from today's $11.2 trillion to $19 trillion in 2016.

The U.S. today makes up about 20% of the world GDP with a $15 trillion economy. Even if the U.S. economy expands by the projected $3.5 trillion during the next five years, this will have its share of the world economic pie drop to 17.7% in 2016.

What Happened to the US Economy?

It may shock you that the Chinese could overtake the U.S. so soon. After all, only ten years ago, the American economy stood at three times larger than that of China's. This was true even though China possesses four times as many people as the United States does. Yet in the last ten years, this dramatic gap has narrowed with astonishing speed.

The United States' economy has still grown most every year in the last decade, besides during the Great Recession. Still, the growth rate has slowed for a variety of reasons. The American economy has gradually lost its competitive edge in this past decade.

The government borrowing and spending at unparalleled levels has acted as a drag on growth. The American regulatory regime has become more crushing under President Obama. Bailouts have cost the nation a fortune. All of these factors have weighed on the U.S. economy during the last decade.

Why is the Economy of China Growing so Fast?

Around 1997 when Great Britain's hundred year lease on Hong Kong expired and they returned it to China, something happened to the Chinese government. Maybe they saw the potential to massively grow their own economy with the addition of the huge economy of Hong Kong.

The communist leadership decided that they should allow the people additional economic freedom. They permitted more capitalism and opened up increasingly free markets. With around a billion and a half citizens now encouraged to work harder to make something for themselves, their economy began to grow rapidly.

Besides this, the Chinese followed two other approaches to vault their economy ahead. They aggressively pursued a policy of stealing technology, patents, and secrets from companies throughout the West. At the same time, they invested the currency that their growing exports earned in overseas corporations and valuable resources on every continent. This has spurred their economic growth and helped to fuel their unprecedented expansion that has raged along at often eleven percent GDP growth per year.

Another thing that the Chinese have done to expand their economy rapidly is to artificially hold down the value of their currency the Yuan. They do not allow the exchange rate to float freely on international markets.

This keeps their exports cheap versus industrial rivals like the US, Japan, Great Britain, and the European Union countries. Through all of these efforts, the Chinese have managed to achieve growth rates not seen in the economically more mature West in around a hundred years.

What are the Consequences for the US?

MarketWatch claims that the date of 2016 when China passes the U.S. economically is a watershed event for the United States. They have called the forecast from the IMF a bombshell that will mark the conclusion of the Age of America. Besides this, they claim that it will be a dark cloud for the U.S. dollar and its huge treasury market.

Newspapers in the United Kingdom have gone further. The Daily Mail claims that the consequences for the U.S. will be a loss of dominant world power status. They even stated that the president who is elected in 2012 will be caretaker for the decline and fall of the U.S.

The Chinese already hold the U.S. hostage today. They have as much as three trillion worth of U.S. dollar holdings that they could begin to dump at any point that it suited them. This would crush the U.S. ability to finance its enormous debts and spending along with the value of the dollar. It would cause damage to the U.S. economy and dollar that would probably never be repaired.

Some analysts claim that this transition of power will lead to a new world order that is run by a handful of power brokers including China's communist leadership. Billionaire currency investor George Soros is one who believes this will come to pass.

This would not be good news for people of the world, as the Chinese government continues to display its brutality and indifference to human life. This stands in marked contrast to the values of liberty, human and property rights, and free markets that both the U.S. and Great Britain before it have embraced and spread around the world.

What will Happen to the Dollar as the World's Reserve Currency?

There is already a lot of quiet discussion on the world that will emerge after the dollar is no longer the reserve currency. The French, Chinese, Russians, and Gulf Oil States have held secret meetings about alternative reserve currencies that the U.S. did not even receive advance notice of or an invitation to attend. Perhaps the last transfer of world reserve currency status is a good example to examine.

The British Empire's economy ceased to be the largest in the world in the early years of the 1900's as America's economy gained ground and overtook it. Yet the pound remained the reserve currency for the world until the end of two world wars, almost fifty years later. This might give the U.S some more time. Do you think the transition from U.S. Dollar to some other reserve currency will take as long?

The Most Valuable Financial Secret In The World

Everyone would like to know the most valuable financial secret in the world. The revelation of this mystery may come as a shock to you. Gold represents the past, present, and future store of value against which all other goods and even currencies have been and will again be measured.

If you can take advantage of this unshakable truth now, then you will profit hugely when the U.S. and other Western nations return to the gold standard in the next decade. In the paragraphs that follow, you will understand why the gold standard has been historically critical, why gold is a timeless store of value that prevents credit and financial collapse, hyperinflation, and currency devaluation, and why the West will soon seek to return to the shelter of its protecting power in only a few short years.

Why Is The Gold Standard So Important?

With a gold standard that backs up a currency, the currency is literally as good as gold. It can only be issued in amounts that correlate with the fixed gold stocks in a nation's vaults.

This is why individuals who are in favor of greater roles of free markets, higher levels of individual responsibility and freedom, and a restriction on government power love money that is backed by gold instead of mere faith and trust in unreliable governments. You simply can not print gold or manipulate its tangible supply, no matter how powerful your government is.

History and Effectiveness of the Modern Age Gold Standard

It may come as a shock to you that for most of their history, the U.S. and Great Britain possessed banking and currency systems that were backed up by gold. Beginning in 1750, the government of King George made it illegal to issue paper money.

The American economy then began to run on silver Spanish pieces of eight and gold coins for bank reserves. This gold standard governed the U.S. and British systems more or less from the years 1750 and 1971.

How well did such a system function? All the way up until President Franklin D. Roosevelt chose to intentionally devalue the dollar in 1933 when he seized control of all gold in the nation, the costs of goods and services remained incredibly stable.

The U.S. dollar's purchasing power remained almost constant over nearly two hundred years. Would that this were the case today, instead of the dollar dropping by fifty percent over the last decade and by a shocking over ninety-seven percent since 1971.

Timeless Store of Value Provides Immunity to Financial Busts

The main reason that gold functions as the greatest financial asset in the world is that it has always maintained its purchasing power throughout all known history. For thousands of years, gold has remained a timeless and globally accepted store of value.

The yellow metal is extraordinarily suited to be a currency after all, since it is rare, divisible, portable, and enduring. To give you an example of how well gold maintains your purchasing power, consider that one hundred years ago a twenty dollar gold piece bought a fine hand crafted suit. Today, the same twenty dollar gold piece will buy you a fine luxury Italian suit.

The great advantage to your currency being backed by this timeless store of value lies in the stability that it provides. Money systems that are backed up by gold are practically impervious to major destabilizing economic boom and bust cycles. This results from the fact that the money and credit supplies are both rigorously regulated by the value of a nation's economy.

A bigger economy translates to more gold, which allows for a larger amount of credit and currency to be extended. This means that the insatiable greed of bankers is not allowed to play havoc with a nation's economy, since they can only make loans out of money based on their tangible gold reserves.

No Way to Protect Savings from Inflation Without Gold Standard

Alan Greenspan once famously wrote that in the absence of the gold standard, you could not keep savings from being diminished by inflation. Money is not a secure store of value without it.

Your savings can be safeguarded against inflation when the currency is backed up by gold.

While there may be other ways to protect the value of your money, such as when you purchase real estate or high quality stocks, there is no better way to protect yourself with liquid and portable real money than with gold.

Excessive Debt Burden Leads to Hyperinflation or Default

Without the gold standard, a nation's debts are allowed to rise to perilous and even unthinkable levels. This is not possible with the gold standard. It is simply a function of the quantity of the country's gold reserves restricting the amount of debt that the nation is able to carry. Bank reserves can only expand in tandem with the size of the economy, which prevents banks from taking on heavy debt loads as well.

Once President Nixon took the U.S. and most of the world off of the gold standard with his actions in 1971, creditors lost their legal rights to the country's gold reserves. At this point, the banks no longer had any limitations to their powers to create new money and credit from thin air, except for the Federal Reserve and its ratios.

The Debt Load Began To Explode

Within years, the debt load began to explode in the U.S. and developed world. The banking system expanded astronomically, since it no longer had to acquire additional gold reserves from greater trade or industrial expansion.

When you consider the actual debt of the U.S. to include unfunded entitlements, the American public debt amounts to a shocking fifty-six trillion dollars. This is nearly four times the size of the country's Gross Domestic Product, or annual total of all goods and services produced in the nation. It also translates to almost seven hundred thousand dollars of debt for every family in the U.S.

These debts can not ever be paid back in today's dollars. This leaves only a few solutions for Western governments that are increasingly desperate. They can default on the debt, which causes the whole economy to fall apart. Alternatively, they can devalue away the unsustainable debts through currency devaluation and the hyperinflation that inevitably results.

One way to do this is to print literally trillions of new dollars. This has been going on at the Federal Reserve since 2007, and it continues unabated today. One day, this will cause the value of the U.S. dollar to collapse. This in turn will lead to runaway hyperinflation, where the prices of goods and services rise from ten to hundreds of percent each month or year.

Once the U.S. money system falls apart because of all of the unchecked debt and money printing that the departure from the gold standard permitted, politicians will finally look at options for what has to replace the fiat paper U.S. dollar.

Is the Gold Standard Still Practical Today?

There will be many pundits, bankers, and politicians who try to convince you and the public that a return to the gold standard is a terrible idea. The reason that bank and government officials will fight the return of gold backed money with all of their collective strength is simple.

Under the rules of the gold backed currency, they will lose most of their incredible power. Money will no longer be created from thin air with the push of a computer button. The money supply will no longer be micro-manageable.

The government will have to live within its means more or less.

Is it practical to talk about a return to the gold standard? The nation has two hundred and sixty-three million troy ounces of gold. With a two trillion dollar money base in dollars, you divide the number of dollars by the nation's gold supply to come up with a gold price of $7,604 per ounce to convert to a currency that is completely backed up by gold.

Is there a living example left for how the gold stand works out nowadays? Switzerland never abandoned the gold standard. The Swiss Franc is still backed up by gold, according to their constitution, to this day. You be the judge. How has their economic stability turned out over the last forty years?

Save Your Financial Assets From The Gathering Storm

If you listen to the financial media much, then you have no doubt heard the almost passionate claims that the U.S. and world economies have recovered from the brink of the disaster that was the financial crisis and Great Recession. Your own personal experiences may tell you otherwise.

Have you ever wondered if the talking heads and politicians are telling you a lie in order to attempt to hold the world economy together as long as possible? The new book "Debt, Deficits, and the Demise of the American Economy" argues the case that the next and by far worst stage of the global economic catastrophe is set to unfold in the future and has already begun.

About the Authors Jeff Cox and Peter J. Tanous

Jeff Cox and Peter J. Tanous wrote this new work "Debt, Deficits, and the Demise of the American Economy" after sharing conversations last year on where the global economy is headed. Jeff Cox is a staff writer for CNBC.com, the financial channel. He has worked as a journalist since 1987. His regular appearances on CNBC TV showcase his market commentaries. Cox's articles are regularly featured on such well known financial sites as Yahoo!, TheStreet.com, and AOL Money.

Co-author Peter Tanous is the President of investment advisory firm Lepercq Lynx. He has worked in the capacity of financial adviser professional for more than forty years. He co-established international investment bank Petra Capital Corporation. Tanous also served as vice president and later international regional director for Smith Barney. Peter Tanous has written a few well regarded books like Investment Gurus and The Wealth Equation.

What is the Premise of the Book?

The bad news is that you have been sold a cruel deception with this idea that the global and U.S. economies are in the midst of a vibrant recovery since 2009. As recently as last August, Alan Greenspan, long time chairman of the Federal Reserve, stated that we now face the dilemma of the most extraordinary financial crisis that he has either read about or personally witnessed. He made this statement a full year after the Great Recession and financial crisis were supposed to have ended.

"Debt, Deficits, and the Demise of the American Economy" picks up with this sobering claim by Alan Greenspan and then takes you the reader on a linear and logical tour of how this crisis happened in the first place and where it is all headed in the bitter end. They call this the most severe financial disaster in all of American history.

The Euro Devaluation Will Continue

The next stages of the financial Armageddon are already beginning today. This involves the utter collapse of the European peripheral countries, which will begin with Greece and next Ireland. The resulting confidence crisis in banks throughout Europe will cause a serious Euro devaluation. You may say that sounds bad for our friends in Europe, but how does it impact the U.S. on a direct level?

As a result of this tragedy in the Eurozone, panic will next break out in stock markets around the world. The violent fear and continuous uncertainty will cause a severe and fast sell off in the global stock exchanges. Then the world bond markets will practically cease to operate and this will cause the interest rates around the globe to soar.

This is when the spotlight will turn to the U.S. Because of the astronomical debt level and runaway deficit spending that we have engaged in here, the panic will spread to the American shores. The Treasury will attempt to pay the debts with freshly printed hundreds of billions of dollars.

As the financial situation declines in the States, investors in the critical U.S. Treasuries markets will lose their necessary confidence to keep buying the U.S. debt. Interest rates in the country will spike. This will lead to a default of a number of states on their municipal debts.

Retirement Payments Will Stop

State offices will also stop sending out retirement payments to the retired state employees. After these events occur, one thing after another will cascade until roaring inflation takes hold on a level not seen in modern America.

This gruesome and depressing situation may sound impossible or at least unlikely to you now.

Once you read this work and learn about the present state of the global financial system, it will not anymore. Authors Cox and Tanous show you that the nonsense being spouted by Washington and New York flies in the face of the cold hard reality.

The final conclusion is a sober one, that the day of reckoning for the years of out of control Federal government spending is about to come due. The book says that we have already walked too far down the road of destruction to even contemplate turning around and retracing our misguided steps. The authors are convinced that a collapse of the global economy will inexorably result.

What Has Caused the Problems?

The authors are certain that the dangers posed by sovereign nations' enormous debts have been grossly underestimated. The U.S. is not immune from this in the least. The fourteen trillion dollar U.S. debt will have to be paid eventually, one way or the other. This puts the world squarely on a crash course with hyperinflation the likes that the country has never personally experienced before.

What Does the Book Predict?

"Debt, Deficits, and the Demise of the American Economy" says that events have already gone too far for us to avoid this next stage of the still unfolding crisis. The authors say that the resulting financial calamity will prove to be worse than what you saw when the financial system collapsed in 2008 to 2009.

First the Euro will collapse, and next the house of cards that is the U.S. debt will fall. In the wake of these twin events, U.S. and world markets will be paralyzed and crushed. They claim that this will happen with the stock market crashing in 2012 or even this very year. There will be runs on all of the banks and an amount of inflation which almost no one is expecting.

What Can You Do to Protect Yourself Personally?

The book does not leave you without solutions. The events that are to come may be unavoidable now, but there is still ample time to protect your finances until the vicious storm finally passes. The authors point out that the traditional allocations in to stocks and bonds will not save you. Instead, you will need to have a major stake in the tested inflation proof assets like gold, silver, oil, timber, and farmland, along with bonds that are inflation protected.

Verdict of the Book

Jeff Cox and Peter Tanous set out to write a book that the person on the street without an economics degree or background could understand. They have succeeded in their efforts to pen the story of how we got here, what the price to pay will be, and how you can save your financial assets from the gathering storm.

The authors expressly state that they do not want to engage in the spread of fear. Instead, they want you the reader to understand what the real bills are that will shortly have to be paid for the extravagance of the last ten years. They believe that foreknowledge allows you to be prepared.

If you want to protect your hard earned money from the ravages of U.S. debt collapse and hyperinflation, then you had best read "Debt, Deficits, and the Demise of the American Economy" and take quick action. The authors provide you with sound strategies for your investments.

They also offer the U.S. government a detailed plan for how to pull the country out of the economic catastrophe once it happens. This makes it required reading for you and your government officials as you prepare for and deal with the global depression that is soon to rear its ugly head.

What could be worse than hearing "I told you so" tomorrow if you have done nothing to protect yourself today?

<u>POLITICS</u>

"Banking and Government Interventions"

Politics

Central Banks Now Buying Gold And Why You Should Too

You may not be aware of the fact that the central banks of the world typically only keep a small percentage of their reserves in gold. In fact, in past decades, they have gradually sold gold holdings. They kept much of the rest of their money in dollars.

From sixty to sixty-five percent of world reserves sit in U.S. dollars, with most of the rest of them in Euros. Yet this trend changed dramatically in the last few years.

In the paragraphs that follow, you will learn why the fact that central banks are now net buyers of gold instead of sellers speaks volumes about the future status and fate of the U.S. dollar as the reserve currency of the world.

How Have Central Banks Changed Their Gold Transactions?

Beginning in 2009, the central banks changed their gold transaction habits. For the full year of 2009, central banks were expected to sell around four million ounces of gold. The actual numbers surprised the investment world. In that year, the central banks of the world actually bought fifteen million ounces of gold.

This represented the first time in many decades where the trend had shifted from central banks as net sellers of gold to net buyers of gold. But 2010's numbers turned even more heads.

Even though the International Monetary Fund sold four hundred and three tons of gold, Central Banks not only purchased all of this, but an additional eighty-seven million ounces of gold on the open markets.

The real central bank gold purchase numbers are almost certainly larger than the official reports indicate. This may come as a surprise to you, but China and Iran especially do not accurately or honestly report their actions with their gold reserves until sometimes years later.

China wishes to make their purchases without causing an impact on the gold prices. Iran is under intense international scrutiny for their illegal atomic weapons program and does not want any one to know what they do with their oil dollars.

What Do Central Banks Use to Pay For their Gold?

Central banks have choices for how they pay when they purchase their gold reserves. They could use their stockpiles of Euros, British Pounds, or Japanese Yen as examples. They do not use these other currencies though. In the vast majority of cases, central banks are buying their larger gold reserves with U.S. dollars.

On the one hand, this makes sense since over half of their reserves are already in dollars. From another perspective, this represents an alarming and disturbing trend to diversify their reserves away from the official reserve currency of the world. Why would central banks, all of whom are players in the U.S. dollar reserve system, choose to do this?

Why Are Banks Buying Gold with Dollars?

A number of the Eurozone economies, governments, and banking systems are on shaky ground.

Greece, Ireland, and now Portugal have all appealed for and received bailouts for their bankrupt governments. In light of this news that is well known, you would think that central banks would be eager to sell their Euros for gold.

Instead of this, recent figures show that central banks have increased their holdings of Euros. Despite the fact there is some uncertainty about the financial situation of some other Euro zone countries including Spain and Italy, the central banks feel more urgently that they must change in their U.S. dollars for gold.

You might be mystified as to why central banks would demonstrate this loss of confidence in the U.S. dollar all of a sudden. There are several reasons that help to explain it. For starters, there is the over fourteen trillion dollars of debt that the United States has amassed. Much of this has been piled on in only the last few years.

Some politicians and economists say that a U.S. debt that amounts to almost one hundred percent of annual gross domestic product, or total value of all goods and services that the country produces every year, is manageable. After all, Japan's debt is still higher by percentage of GDP. Even so, this massive U.S. debt is the largest amount by sheer numbers in the history of the modern world.

Besides this, with an annual deficit, or budget shortfall, of over a trillion dollars for three years in a row that is now up to almost one and a half trillion dollars, the debt will only continue to climb in the years that come. This gives central banks cause for concern about the value of their U.S. debt that is denominated in dollars. China and Japan, the two largest holders of this debt, are especially wary and even concerned.

A more disturbing reason for the loss of central bank confidence in the dollar revolves around the number of dollars in existence in the world today. The U.S. Treasury and Fed have worked hard together to increase the quantity of dollars by over three hundred percent since 2007/2008 alone.

They have done this through printing more money electronically, by buying treasury bonds and bills at auctions, and by extending dollar swap lines to other central banks during the financial crisis to increase global dollar liquidity. The end result is that you see simply too many U.S. dollars floating around both at home and abroad.

These two effects of too much U.S. dollar denominated debt and way too many dollars period together cause governments and central banks to distrust the dollar. Nations with large dollar reserves are beginning to panic. This helps to explain why the dollar has declined sharply against all other major currencies, as well as gold, in the first quarter of 2011.

What Do Central Banks' Gold Sales Mean for the Long Term Gold Prices?

Until even a few years ago, central banks were net sellers of gold. This helped to keep gold prices down. The belief that they were still sellers slowed the prices from truly skyrocketing as investors panicked around the world during the financial crisis and Great Recession.

Now that they have turned the tables and begun purchasing gold, central banks have radically altered the equation of gold buyers and sellers in the world. Because of their changed perceptions of the dollar, this trend will likely continue.

There are projections that central banks will attempt to purchase as many as two hundred to two hundred fifty tons of gold on the open market in London in 2011. You can expect this to continue to support gold prices over both the near and long term.

How high might this activity push gold prices over the next few years? Jim Rogers is a legendary American currency and commodities investor, author, and fund manager. He projects gold prices will rise to $2,000 per ounce and probably much higher this decade. John Paulson runs one of the largest hedge funds in the world. He believes that the same dollar based inflation that central banks fear will drive gold to between $2,400 and $4,000 per ounce in the next few years.

If there is even a possibility that central banks will lose complete faith in the dollar in the upcoming years, should you not purchase at least some gold with your investment portfolio and savings to protect your other dollar based assets from these very real threats?

Is the Silver Price Manipulated By Banks And Government?

The first week of May's blood bath in the silver market has raised the suspicions of some analysts and traders. You may or may not have heard the word manipulation thrown around.

This shockingly fast decline of silver by nearly thirty percent in less than a week conjures up memories of unfair price manipulation in the market that has gone on before.

In the following paragraphs, you will read about the possible players who are trying to keep a lid on the rapid silver price appreciation that has been overdue for literally decades.

What Factors Could Have Caused A Pullback in Silver Prices?

You might start by asking yourself is this pullback manipulation of the silver markets at all? There have been numerous attempts to explain why silver would fall off of a cliff after months and months of steady and sometimes breathtaking gains.

The fundamentals for silver are certainly real and present. Industry heavily demands it, as do investors who look for a so called poor man's alternative to gold to hedge against anticipated inflation and currency debasement by the governments of the U.S. and the West.

There was big news over the weekend of May first that some have used as an excuse for silver's fall. Al Qaeda mastermind Bin Ladin was finally killed, and this sparked at least a temporary rally in the dollar. Some who hold silver and gold as protection against uncertainty in the world may believe that this reduced the need for the precious metals.

The truth is that the terrorist situation is more dangerous than ever now in the wake of the martyring of the head of the greatest worldwide terrorist organization. Silver and gold should be up not down on the news.

Others have said that a correction in silver was long overdue. After all, the metal did rise over eighty percent since the end of 2011. That might explain some of the price action, but corrections tend to be in the neighborhood of ten percent, not the almost thirty percent that silver suffered.

Still other pundits have claimed that softer economic data that showed slowing economic growth around the U.S. and world is to blame. Since silver is heavily used as an industrial metal, a decline in future world growth might affect its demand and prices some. Once again, this does not warrant such a steep fall in the price. This idea also completely leaves out the significant reconstruction needs in Japan.

Could The CME Group Have Manipulated the Price of Silver?

The Chicago Mercantile Exchange group is the largest operator of futures markets in the world. Silver is heavily traded via paper contracts in large five thousand ounce quantities on their commodities trading floors.

The CME is able to influence the amount of these contracts that investors buy and hold when they raise the margin rates. Beginning on April 25th and extending through ten days that led up to the massive drop in silver prices, the CME raised the minimum margin requirements five separate times. On some exchanges, this caused the margin percentage that you have to keep for each contract to rise from three to nine percent.

The Comex exchange in New York that the CME owns became the latest to raise its silver margins by eighty-four percent on May ninth. These moves had a measurable effect on open silver positions, as investors closed out fifteen percent of their open interest in silver since the exchanges began to enact these higher margin minimums.

Why Would the CME Potentially Manipulate the Price of Silver?

Naturally the Chicago Mercantile Exchange has a defense for why it has raised margins by such an astonishing amount in less than two weeks. They claim that because of previously unseen amounts of volatility, they had to do something.

In order to protect investors from the higher levels of risk that they face, the CME says it raises the margin amounts that it requires. What makes this argument suspicious is that they continued to raise the rates until they crashed the price and wiped out many of the same silver investors that they claimed they were trying to protect.

There is another argument for why the CME would go through the trouble to stop the run up by any means necessary. They may have been coerced to do this by the Federal Reserve or other elements of the U.S. government. There is historical precedent for government interference in the silver markets and their price that goes back to only the early 1980's.

Why Would the Government Want to Manipulate the Price of Silver?

Neither the CME nor the U.S. government will have forgotten what happened when the Hunt Brothers attempted to corner the silver market back in the early 1980's. The price of silver rapidly climbed to over $50 per ounce before the Federal Reserve and the commodities exchanges stepped in to force them to unwind their positions.

Silver is priced like gold primarily in U.S. dollars. The American government will not let silver as an alternative currency run too far, too fast. This is because when precious metals rapidly appreciate, it means that the dollar is aggressively depreciating.

Gradual depreciation of the dollar they can and do accept, but too much in a short period of time would lead to hyperinflation, or prices of goods and services that rise astronomically, and possible dollar collapse.

Who Controls Large Amounts of Silver and Could Manipulate the Prices?

There are two noteworthy men in particular who held large silver positions until the crash in prices began. One of them is the richest man on earth, Carlos Slim. The other is George Soros, the famous commodities and currency investor. Both of these men sold off large silver positions as the price started to come down.

You might ask if this qualifies as manipulation. Their actions caused other investors to scurry for the exits, and this played a part in the silver price route. If they took profits at the peak and then purchase their silver holdings back again at a much lower price, then they become more complicit in price manipulation, since their actions could move the markets.

Has the Silver Bull Market Come to An End in Light of the Prices Crashing?

If you are a silver investor, you may be worried that this dramatic price action signals an end to silver's historic run. Nothing could be farther from the truth. The weakness in the dollar is a major part of the run up in both silver and gold, and this has not changed at all since the correction began in May.

If anything, the Fed has convinced more investors that they simply can not raise rates any time soon because of the weak economy and the enormous government debt loads that they must service at the interest rates that they set. Fears of inflation from the Fed's continuous dollar printing have also not been diminished.

The rally in silver can not begin to stop until three things happen. The instability in the world that surrounds the Middle East will have to go away. The ongoing multiple year investigation of perceived silver market manipulation by the silver bullion banks led by JP Morgan Chase will have to be completed. Most of all, the Federal Reserve will have to aggressively raise interest rates.

Does it look to you like these factors will all come together any time soon?

The Major Key That Keeps People And The World in Poverty

If you have ever considered the plight of the poor, then you may wonder why there is not enough money in the world for everybody. The answer to this question may surprise you.

Interest is actually the major problem that exists in the money system to keep people in poverty around the world today.

It may shock you to learn that this flawed system that charges people for the use of money did not always exist. In fact, interest has become the dominant factor that splits people into rich and poor today. In the paragraphs that follow, you will learn what interest is, how and why it was not always charged, how it divides the rich and the poor, and how economies can actually thrive without it.

What Is Interest?

The simple dcfinition of interest is a fee that borrowers pay to lenders in order to use the lenders' money or assets. Although there are many things that you can pay interest on, you usually find that people pay it for borrowed money.

The institution or person who loans the money receives this interest as payment for the use of these money assets.

Interest is usually charged and expressed as a percentage of the amount that is borrowed. This fee that has to be repaid on top of the original principal is known as the interest rate.

Interest also has deeper, more subtle explanations. It is payment given to the person or institution that loans out money for taking a credit risk, or chance that they will not receive their original money back. It is also compensation for a lender's opportunity cost, when they pass on alternative investments that they might have made instead with the money that they loaned.

You the borrower are supposed to be grateful that you have the use of the assets now, instead of being forced to wait to obtain them in the future on your own. Obviously, the lender is happy to enjoy the often considerable fee of even twenty percent or higher for the privilege that you gain when you have the money now.

They call this interest the price of credit. What makes interest even more lucrative for the lender and more disadvantageous for the borrower is that interest is usually compounded, or it grows at a rate that is exponential as it accrues not only on the original money loaned, but also on the interest that has already accrued.

Where and Why Was Interest Forbidden In the Past?

This idea that you can charge for the use of money is actually a fairly recent construct. In the Middle Ages, both the Catholic world and the Islamic lands looked down on the concept of interest. The Catholic Church first condemned it at the Second Lateran Council. Later at the Council of Vienna, they forbade the practice of this usury and went a step further to say that any legislation that permitted interest was heresy.

From 1179, if you charged interest in the world of Western Christendom, then you were excommunicated and cast out of the church and society. The ruling class in Western Europe learned to shun this practice of interest as something that was morally reprehensible. Loans were generally made to help those in a bad situation, such as to those who had suffered from fires, poor harvests, or from other natural disasters.

Since no goods were created when money was lent out, the general belief was that you should not receive compensation for the act. The vast lands of Islam that stretched from North Africa to India and Indonesia went along with this reasoning and heavily discouraged the practice of usury as well. Their scholars within the Islamic world claimed that the Qur'an forbade the concept of interest.

How Does Interest Split People into Rich and Poor?

Now that you know how interest operates and that it was not always an accepted practice, you should also understand that today the practice of interest serves to divide people into two classes, those of rich and poor. The rich learn early on in life that their money comes from the miracle of compound interest and similar types of investments.

This simply means that they can accumulate wealth much smarter and faster, not through hard work, but when they use the concept of interest to grow their money over time at these compound interest rates.

Not only does this interest money benefit from lower tax rates of no more than fifteen percent, it also creates a positive cash flow that they can continue to invest.

Thanks to compound interest, the rich are constantly growing richer at the same time that poor people are simply struggling to keep their heads above water.

Poor people are not familiar with the compound interest ability to double your money every four to seven years. They may have heard of the term, but they usually end up on the receiving end of the interest equation as the ones who pay it on car loans, credit card bills, mortgages, and other personal loans.

They may work hard and try to use their money wisely, but they have the tax system that works against them, and charges them often twice as high tax penalties on their work earned money as the rich pay on their investments and earned interest.

The poor do not have the benefit or knowledge to collect interest. No one bothered to teach them about it in the first place. Instead, they pay it out to the rich, and it represents a constant drain on their monthly finances.

How Do Economies Thrive When There is No Interest?

It may be hard to imagine a world without interest, but the absence of interest does not mean that you can not have a booming economy. The reality is quite the opposite. In the late Middle Ages and early Renaissance years, commerce managed to thrive and the economies expand even though interest was not used on a wide scale.

The merchants of Holland and Great Britain plied their trades and sailed their ships around the world. This is in part because they did not put their money into the enslaving pool of interest. Instead, they put their money to work on trade and commerce.

Imagine a world where there are reduced barriers to obtain money. Instead of being limited by the restrictions enforced now when you obtain and pay back borrowed money with interest, you would be free to easily obtain and put money to work to start a business. Since there would not be incentive to leave money to work in banking pools, the money would all be put to work productively.

More goods and services would be produced. Trade would expand and flourish as it did in the Islamic lands and Western Europe at the end of the Middle Ages and Renaissance times. Best of all, every person who was enterprising would have the same opportunity to borrow money and put it to use in order to better themselves. This worked well three hundred to five hundred years ago, and it would work for the modern economies of today too.

Can you think of a better way to stimulate the stricken Western economies than by freeing up the creative talents and energies of the vast numbers of people who are held down by the force of interest to this day?

Debunking Government's Tweaking on Economic Numbers

Have you ever read a government economic statistic and wondered why the number seems to good to be true based on your own personal and business experience? Consider the unemployment rate as one example.

The official rate now stands at just under nine percent. Yet one in five American households reports that they have a member who is out of work and actively seeking a job.

Another statistic that looks suspicious every time you go to the grocery store is the famed CPI, or consumer price index. According to the government report, today inflation is basically non-existent at under a percent a year.

This is only true if you do not buy groceries, clothes, gasoline, utility services, or any number of other routine weekly needs. If you are the one in the family who pays the bills and does the shopping, then you know that something is wrong with these inflation numbers, since your actual costs are up more like five, ten, or even twenty percent in the last year or so.

There is a site and service that acts as a watch dog on the government reports and official statistics. It is called Shadow Statistics.

Shadow stats makes its home on the Internet at shadowstats.com, where you can find out what the real numbers are on these various economic indicators. Its mission is to debunk the masterful U.S. government's tweaking and outright manipulation of official statistics.

What Exactly is Shadow Statistics?

Shadow Government Statistics is a service that John Williams puts together. This electronic newsletter analyzes, reports on, and exposes manipulations and weaknesses in the present day financial information that the American government reports. It also monitors various private sector data numbers. The service furthermore offers an unbiased and honest appraisal of the real financial and economic situation facing the United States, without giving in to political considerations and governmental bias.

When Did the U.S. Government Begin to Fix The Data Releases?

It was only in the years after World War II that the U.S. government began to offer up routine reports on the economy. This is when they started to publish the CPI, the GNP and GDP, and the unemployment rate. Only a few years after the government made these statistics available, they began to manipulate them.

They did this by changing the formulas for the key data.

Both Republican and Democrat Presidents were guilty of this practice going back to the Nixon era. President Carter's administration was the first one that got caught actively manipulating statistics.

They were seen intentionally under reporting the actual inflation rate. Does that sound familiar to you today?

It only continued from this point forward with every subsequent President. President Reagan's administration changed the formulas to boost the all important GNP and GDP growth numbers. The first President Bush worked to systematically lower the CPI inflation numbers. His administration also manipulated the GDP number in an effort to try to win reelection in the failed attempt of 1992.

President Bill Clinton is responsible for the death of the last reliable statistic, the sacred unemployment numbers. These had been consistently reported since before even the Great Depression, when they peaked around twenty-five percent at the worst point. Clinton and his camp found a way to take five million discouraged workers off of the roles of official unemployment statistics.

The unemployment rate has never been accurate since. The formulas for reporting poverty were altered. The CPI inflation numbers were tweaked once more to lower the official inflation figures. President Clinton's team also overstated GDP growth.

The second President Bush continued and expanded President Clinton's tricky redefining of long established formulas for government data releases. They artificially reduced the CPI inflation numbers. At the same time, they began using seasonal adjustments to make the unemployment numbers look lower and the GDP look higher than they actually are.

How Do These Manipulations of Data Practically Affect the Actual Numbers?

The government altered the GDP formulas for determining the economic growth in the country after 1980.

Using the 1980 numbers, today's GDP is three percentage points overstated. Inflation is around three to five percentage points understated. Most shockingly, the unemployment rate is stated at less than half of what it should be.

Actual unemployment today is far closer to twenty percent than it is to the nine percent that Washington is desperate for you to believe.

Are Americans Aware of this Government Manipulation of the Data?

The Kaiser Foundation has taken surveys in the past that demonstrated that Americans like you are not completely fooled by the numbers. In your heart, you know that something is wrong in a country that is supposed to be in the middle of a massive economic recovery.

The average American today believes that unemployment and inflation are much higher than the official statistics reveal. You also know that real economic growth proves to be far weaker in practice than the optimistic three to five percent numbers that the government commonly throws around.

Shadow Statistics lays the official deceptions bare. The reason for the disparity between official economic data and public misperception is simple. It shows you that government statistics are rooted in politically expedient bias. These have continuously drifted away from your real experience and the economic truth at an increasing pace since the middle of the 1980's.

Unemployment and inflation numbers are intentionally under reported. Economic information and employment numbers are over reported on purpose. This is partly because the U.S. government has come to recognize the critical role of consumer confidence.

With two-thirds of the U.S. economy based on consumer spending, the government relies on the consumers' perception of reality in order to bolster the still-sagging economic picture that has never really rebounded since the Great Recession and financial crisis began in 2007.

What Factors Does Shadow Statistics Especially Look Out for in Government Statistics Reporting?

Seasonal adjustments are one factor that the government uses to fudge the data. They employ them officially in an effort to eliminate noise and distortion that happen every year because of holidays, weather, and other seasonal factors. This could be a legitimate process, except for the fact that the government often struggles with the adjustments and their applications to the data. Unemployment claims on a weekly basis and seasonal employment data are two components that simply do not adjust accurately.

The kind of growth is another area of which you should be wary. Growth can be reported on a month to month basis, year over year basis, or annual basis. The government generally relies on month to month statistic changes. Quarter over quarter is sometimes utilized too. More honest and appropriate measurements would be compared on a year to year change basis. This would also serve to cut out seasons' noise.

Finally, revisions can be tricky. The majority of the government released economic figures are frequently and routinely revised. This can cause monthly numbers to appear weaker or stronger when they are revised. Yet two of the most important numbers are not revised at all. These are the unemployment rate and the CPI inflation index. The new data series are often not fairly able to be compared to the older ones, especially as the agencies make changes to the formula. Despite this, the financial media rarely bother to report on it.

In the end, you will have to decide who you will believe. In light of past deceptions that Republican and Democratic Presidents and their administrations have all made, do you believe President Obama's administration numbers on unemployment and inflation to be more correct, or the personal experience that you see playing out all around you every day?

Why Working Hard Gets You Penalized With High Taxes

When you were growing up, you were probably taught that you can achieve great success and wealth in America if you work hard. This is the mantra that built this country over the centuries, after all. The truth is, a better motto for you to guide your life and finances by any more is to work smarter, not harder.

This is because the tax system in the United States favors investments, and especially smart particular types of investments, far more than it does income that is considered by the IRS and Treasury Department to be earned. In the following paragraphs, you will come to understand why this was not always the case, as the present day income tax system only came into effect in 1943 in the middle of World War II.

Today's Tax System - The Current Tax Payment Act of 1943

Today, employees receive their pay checks, salaries, and wages after they have already paid their taxes. You may not think about it this way, but the truth is that the government collects what it believes you owe them directly at the source, before it ever reaches your hands. You may shrug your shoulders and say that it has always been like that, but this is far from the truth.

In the first hundred and fifty years plus of the United States' history, income taxes were not usually withheld from citizens' paychecks. Up until 1943, most of the time the government did not bother to enforce pre-payment like this unless they had a dire need for additional revenue. Only in 1862 during the administration of President Abraham Lincoln did you first see income taxes of any kind collected. He found himself in an expensive Civil War that had to be financed.

After the Civil War, the government abolished the income tax withholding system as well as the new income tax entirely in 1872.

In 1913, the income tax became permanent with the ratification of the sixteenth amendment to the Constitution. This tax appeared in order to finance World War I. The tax withholding scheme only lasted until 1917, by which time the complaints of employers prevailed upon Congress to repeal it. At the time, the burden on businesses to act as both businessmen and tax collectors was considered to be excessive.

Once the Social Security Act came into effect under President Franklin D. Roosevelt, and Social Security taxes began to be taken from paychecks, the die had been cast for a permanent income tax withholding system to be enforced.

The Current Tax Payment Act enacted in 1943 used the justification of World War Two's hefty costs to force the pre-payment burden back on to the American people. This time, income tax changed from one that only the wealthy and high earning citizens had to pay to one that rich and poor alike paid.

These tax rates were so much higher in 1943 that the government did not feel confident that it would be able to effectively collect the income taxes from Americans at the end of the year. They knew that by withholding the heavy levies at the payroll source, they could be certain that their money was not spent by the citizens in the normal course of the year.

Milton Friedman is the economist who came up with the 1943 tax withholding system. Ironically, the man who created this onerous system on behalf of his employer the Treasury later bitterly regretted his part in setting it up.

Only a few retirees today remember the time when taxes were not withheld from your paycheck up front. Back up until 1943, you simply paid all of your income taxes that were due either on March 15th, or in installments that you made quarterly, if you preferred.

Now if you are a regular employee, you never see your earned income that comprises your taxes. The only workers who still realize the benefit of the pre-1943 withholding system are the independent contractors. Their taxes are not taken out in advance.

Instead, they may be paid quarterly, as with the original income tax collection system. Unfortunately, independent contractors are penalized with double social security tax rates, since they have no "employers" to share in the heavy burden.

How Does Income Tax Affect Your Income Today?

Today's income tax system affects your income in three different ways. The effects disadvantage money that you actually work for over money that you invest or gain through passive income.

While you might think that the government is concerned for the poor working man, the truth is that earned income is most heavily penalized by the tax system put in place back in 1943.

Earned Income Gets the Highest Penalty

It may seem counter intuitive, but in the information age that you now find yourself, the government does not at all reward hard work. The tax code allows for as much as fifty percent of your income to be taken in Federal and state income taxes. While the top tax bracket for Federal taxes maxes out at 39.6%, there are also state income taxes in most states to consider.

Between them, a full half of the earned income that you work for is taken from you. This represents the most heavily taxed type of income that you can possibly make. It is a certainty that the harder you work, the more taxes you will pay. Not only this, but you will pay a higher percentage rate of taxes on your earnings as they rise.

Portfolio Income is Taxed at Less Than Half The Earned Income Rate

If you instead spend your time working to build up intelligent investments in a portfolio with stocks, bonds, or mutual funds, then you will find that your investments' tax rate is less than half as much as on money that you work to earn.

Both capital gains and dividends are taxed at a maximum rate of from fifteen to twenty percent. On lower to middle income brackets, these portfolio incomes that you hold a year or longer are often not taxed at all these days. The moral of the story is clear. Portfolio income is significantly advantaged by the tax code over traditional worked for and earned income.

Passive Income Can be Earned Tax Free

You may be shaking your head at the idea of making money that does not require any taxes at all. It is true; there are forms of passive income that accrue tax free. Passive incomes are those incomes that you receive through particular types of investments where you do not materially participate.

If you own a business that you do not actively manage but are a limited partner in, then this is counted as passive income. Some passive income can even be earned without taxes being applied because of all of the tax breaks associated with them. Investments in oil and gas exploration and producing properties are some of these. The government rewards the efforts to find domestic energy sources.

Residential and commercial income properties are two other types of passive income investments that can be brought in without the need to pay taxes. This is because the government chooses to encourage and reward people who provide housing for the general population. They also favor those who provide premises where businesses can operate. In either case, you are able to earn a significant percentage return income on your investment, often completely tax free.

Now that you understand the way that the income tax system works, ask yourself a simple but powerful question. Which form of income makes the most sense in the information age - earned income, portfolio income, or certain passive incomes? Leave your comments below.

The Sovereign Debt Crisis in America is Now Official

If you have flipped through the news channels or picked up a newspaper lately, then you will have probably seen a headline that sounds ominous - S&P downgrades the outlook on U.S. debt and public finances to negative.

You may not grasp exactly what this warning means, but it is something that you should understand. One financial network anchor has called this the beginning of the sovereign debt crisis in America.

The implications of this judgment call on the finances of the government of the United States are profound. When you read the subsequent paragraphs, you will understand why they will probably affect everything from the government's ability to borrow money cheaply to your ability to have a low interest rate on your mortgage and other debt.

What Exactly Happened with the S&P Downgrade to U.S. Financial Outlook?

You should understand how important it is that the United States has a stable financial outlook and Triple A credit rating, the best one possible. The U.S. has held its AAA credit rating for one hundred and twenty continuous years.

The ratings agencies and other countries around the world have respected the United States as the gold standard for debt and financial management for much of this time. The fact that the dollar is the reserve currency of the world has helped the country to maintain this critically important credit rating.

This highest of credit ratings and stable outlook allows the United States to borrow money at ridiculously low interest rates. In some cases, they are under a percent per year. The U.S. has been able to borrow tremendous amounts of money over the past ten years because of this ultra low interest rate on the government debt.

But something has begun to change with the S&P credit rating agency's opinion of the stability of the U.S. debt and government finances. Back on January 14th, both S&P and Moody's Investors Service sounded the alarm that the U.S. could lose its triple A credit rating if the country continues to boost the national debt.

On April 18, the Standard & Poor's ratings agency made good on its previous threat and reduced the outlook for the country's credit rating to negative. This has never before happened to the U.S. in the over twenty years that the S&P awarded outlooks to a country. Up to this point, the U.S. has always earned the stable rating.

Why Did S&P Lower the Outlook for U.S. Debt Ratings?

S&P continued the stern rebuke when it stated that there is at least a one third chance that the United States' government debt will lose its Triple A standard that is has enjoyed for more than a century. You should know that there are several reasons that S&P cited. They are most concerned about the government's inability to effectively deal with the long and medium term budget challenges over the next two years.

S&P made particular reference to the fact that the U.S. is the only major Western economy that has not cut spending and raised taxes in an effort to reduce its debt. Instead, the government continues to run ever greater deficits than in the years before. Two years after the financial crisis began, the leaders in Washington have not been able to come together to determine a way to turn around the country's deteriorating finances.

S&P notes that there are other long term financial problems too, such as Social Security and Medicare deficits that loom in the future.

If you look deeper into the ratings agency's report, they are also concerned about other issues that the U.S. faces. They point to the housing market decline and problems that the nation has not resolved. They also reference potential major upcoming defaults in the trillion dollar student loan market. All of these issues played a part in their decision.

How Does the U.S. Negative Outlook Compare to Other Major Economies?

You may have heard that other Western countries Greece, Ireland, and Portugal have had their outlooks and subsequently credit ratings cut. This does not give the U.S. excuse to justify its own downgrade. Other major economic powers like Britain, Canada, France, Australia, Germany, and even the tiny island of Guernsey in the Channel Islands all have superior credit ratings with stable outlooks.

What are the Impacts on the U.S. Government?

Right after the S&P outlook cut, you saw the interest rates that the U.S pays for its debt rise sharply. These Treasury yields eventually calmed back down, but it was still an alarming sign. This is because the U.S. has fourteen trillion in debt on which it pays interest.

A tiny one tenth of one percent increase in the interest rate would amount to billions more tacked on to the deficit in just a little time. Should you actually see the United States suffer a credit rating downgrade, then the expense when the government rolls the debts will go up substantially. This would make an already bad debt situation for the U.S. even worse in the future.

Potential Impacts For Investors and the U.S. Economy

There are a range of damages that would be done to the U.S. economy if the credit rating is actually cut. Studies show that the stock market would drop at least six percent and maybe even ten percent in a matter of months if this tragic event occurs.

The dollar would also suffer additional declines at a faster than usual pace as foreign investors begin to sell their U.S. government debt holdings and repatriate their dollars to home currencies. Trade might even be impacted if foreigners begin to believe that the U.S. will not make good on its legendary trade imbalances, or difference between the amount of goods that we buy and sell abroad.

Potential Impacts for the Consumer

So far you have read about debt downgrade impacts on a large scale.

It is certainly upsetting to think that the U.S. government might struggle to pay its bills and that the economy as a whole could suffer. There are impacts on you as a consumer that could result from this outlook downgrade and any impending national debt downgrade too.

The government treasury yields have a big effect on the interest rates that you pay for loans and credit. This not only means that credit cards' and car loans' interest rates would go up, but also mortgage rates on houses would rise. This hits you in your ability to finance purchases of any kind besides cash.

How can You Protect Yourself from the U.S. Outlook Downgrade?

Your dollars have dropped in value since the U.S. outlook was downgraded. This decreases the real value of practically any investment that you hold, such as stocks, bonds, mutual funds, and even real estate that are all denominated in dollars.

There are a few investments that you can look to for protection against this new American debt crisis. Gold posted a fresh series of all time highs on the heels of the S&P outlook downgrade for the U.S. Silver also reached a new three decade high at the same time.

Uncertainty and dollar devaluation always benefit the precious metals. Can you think of a better time to invest a part of your savings and investment portfolio in either or both of these two safe havens than now?

Millions in Government Grants You Never Have to Repay

Have you ever seen one of those exciting television commercials that promises you millions of dollars in government grants that you will never have to repay? As shady as those may seem on the surface, such ads are really not fraud.

The U.S. Federal Government runs several grant programs that enable individuals like you to achieve your dreams as they offer real money that does not have to be repaid for the use of college, opening a small business, purchasing a house, paying off bills, and other activities.

In the article below, you will learn all about these government grants that actually do not have to be paid back and about how USGrantSource.org is able to help you to obtain these funds in the simplest way possible.

How Is It Possible to Obtain Such Grant Funds?

The claim that USGrantSource.org makes to be able to assist you in obtaining such grants has been well documented by multiple respected news sources. Their program has been seen on such networks as ABC, NBC, CNN, FOX, and CBS.

If you have U.S. citizenship, then you really can qualify to get even tens of thousands of dollars from the state, Federal, and local governments, as well as privately run foundations. You will not have to demonstrate a high credit score, put up collateral, or even repay these monies if you qualify to receive them.

Why Would the Government Give Away this Money in the First Place?

You may wonder why the government would add to the budget deficit and growing public debt by giving away money to U.S. citizens. The simple answer is that the present administration wants to pump up the faltering American economy. One of the ways that they attempt to increase consumer spending is through offering this financial assistance to individuals like yourself.

The Federal government is interested in helping you to reach your goals and dreams. This is to their benefit as well. If you open up a business that helps you to employ other people and earn money to pay taxes, they gain.

If you go to college or a trade school on a grant and then obtain a higher paying job as a result, then you will pay substantially higher taxes to the government's ultimate benefit. This explains why they are willing to make a relatively small investment in you now so that you can pay them back many times over in the longer time frame of your working life.

What is Required of You To Get These Government Grants?

You may think that there is some hidden catch to this too good to be true sounding offer.

No one just shows up at your household with a check for ten thousand dollars. It is true that some initiative is required on your part to get this money.

You must track down the available opportunities, get the requisite information and forms, make application for the program that fits your unique situation, and then correspond with the agency to make certain that you meet their continuing criteria in order to successfully land such a government grant.

The first step in your quest to actually hold a no strings attached government grant check in your hands is to go to the website USGrantSource.org. Once you are on their site, you will be able to answer a few simple questions that will tell you if you qualify for any of this free money that your Uncle Sam is actually just giving away.

Once you qualify for their program, USGrantSource.org will assist you in tracking down the best matching funding programs for you personally. They will not only help you to locate the one that fit your particular scenario best, but they will walk you through each and every one of the steps that is a part of the application process.

How Can this Program Help You to Obtain Free Money

It will probably shock you to learn that there are literally tens of thousands of different funding sources and programs that are available to you every year. The USGrantSource.org site takes all of the mystery and guess work out of the process of determining the programs that exist and are best suited for your situation.

The site's database is loaded with thousands of different funding possibilities. These are updated on a weekly basis with additional opportunities. Besides this, the USGrantSource.org gives you training modules that include secrets only the grant insiders know. These will show you the precise means to successfully apply for funds so that you can count on receiving the greatest number of government checks possible.

What Does the USGrantSource.org Accelerated Funding Offer You?

The kit and site show you all of the grants for which you are qualified. They go through thousands of different public and private grants that pay thousands of dollars each in their database to do this. They then shepherd you along the sometimes difficult process in order to ensure that you get your applications done properly and on time.

They provide you with contacts that you would not find on your own. The step by step process is proprietary and proven to work. This makes certain that you qualify for and obtain grants as quickly as possible. This site and program guarantees that you have the greatest possible odds to obtain the funding that you both require and deserve.

How Come This Site and Program are So Reasonably Priced?

The makers of the USGrantSource.org acknowledge that the economy is still as bad as it has been since the Great Depression eighty years ago.

Because individuals like yourself who need the help are so deserving but possibly unable to afford an expensive membership, they have worked to make this one of the most affordable programs around.

They give you a three day trial membership for only a dollar. After that, the monthly subscription fee defaults to a reasonable $67.21 for every thirty days. This helps to cover the costs of the program and to keep the website up to date and running smoothly and efficiently. You can cancel at any time that you like.

The Money Back Guarantee If You Are Not Fully Satisfied

Many of you may still be unsure if this grant program will really work out for you just as it is advertised and reviewed. The owners of the USGrantSource.org are sympathetic towards your natural skepticism. That is why they offer a full sixty day money back guarantee program. The guarantee is simple and effective.

If you try the Accelerated Grant Kit program for the sixty days and then you decide that you are not one hundred percent thrilled with the results, then you can contact them by email or phone and count on a refund of all the money that you have paid so far. They will not ask you any questions as to why. On top of this refund, you will be allowed to hold on to all of the kit materials for the future.

When there is no longer any risk involved with trying out the grant program, what is stopping you from proactively taking hold of your dreams and making them a reality?

Will Gold And Silver Become Legal Tender Again In The US?

With all the constant talk that you hear about the unsustainable U.S. government debt, declining dollar, and enormous budget imbalances, it should not come as a surprise to you that gold and silver are becoming more popular as investment vehicles every day.

The latest news about the precious metals is more startling still. Gold and silver are now actually legal tender alongside plain old paper greenbacks in part of the United States. Read on to learn where this has occurred, the reasons that this is important, and why it is bad news for the Federal government and the IRS.

Who Has Legalized Using Gold and Silver as Money?

This very month of June, the state of Utah set a precedent as the first in the union to declare that gold and silver coins are legal currency. More importantly, this action looks like it will not be limited to Utah alone.

Minnesota just followed in Utah's foot steps and has moved one step nearer to approving both gold and silver coins as legal money. Montana has talked seriously about legalizing gold and silver for a few years now. Right now, Idaho, North Carolina, and another nine state at least are in the process of drafting bills that make gold and silver legal as real money within their state jurisdictions.

This movement has even gained traction on a national level, as one Republican congressman in Washington has put forward a bill to look into the possibility of accepting gold and silver as concurrent legal tender alongside the U.S. dollar on a national scale.

What is the Precedent of Gold and Silver As Legal Tender in the U.S.?

Throughout most of human history, gold and silver were treated as real money. In fact, practically all currencies were struck in silver preferably, or gold alternatively. This was also the case in the U.S. with the silver and gold coins such as the famed twenty dollar gold piece.

Other smaller U.S. coinage was mostly struck on about ninety percent silver composition blanks until the year 1965, when it was famously and permanently debased in favor of less expensive metals.

Until 1971, all U.S. dollars were legally exchangeable for gold under the gold standard. This golden rule had dominated American monetary reality throughout most of American history, with interruptions under President Franklin D. Roosevelt who made it illegal for Americans to own gold in his famous gold seizure act of 1933.

It was President Nixon who ended dollar to gold convertibility finally forty years ago. The result has been a breath taking decline of over ninety-five percent in the value of the dollar to gold or silver.

The Legal Tender Rulings on Gold and Silver Are Significant

The reason that it matters what governments allow you to use for currency is that governments are the ones who control the definition of the word currency in its entirety.

Since the Federal government has decreed that it will only accept paper money in payments of debts, this has caused you and previous generations of Americans to believe that money is green paper bills that you carry around in your wallet or deposit in the bank.

This money has no intrinsic value in and of itself. It is only accepted as a medium of exchange because the government declares that paper is the only money that you can use.

But now, thanks to the efforts of the great state of Utah, and soon to be Minnesota, Montana, and other states, the Federal Reserve Bank and officials in Washington are under severe challenge. Since Utah will now accept state tax payments in gold and silver coins, the Federal government is losing its monopolistic control over what can and can not be used as exclusive currency within the borders of the United States.

Granted, Utah is only one small state, but as the other states begin to move in this direction as is already happening, the pressure on the Federal Government to accept a dual monetary standard of both precious metal coins and paper dollars will mount.

Eventually, this will lead to the Federal government caving in on the issue of gold and silver as real currency. When this happens, watch out. The days of the dollar are already numbered, thanks to the gross mismanagement of the paper currency by the Feds over the last four to five years in particular. When people are given a free choice of using tangible real money such as gold and silver coins over paper dollars that drop in value all of the time and long term, they will choose the real coins in most cases.

What Are the Government Penalties that Discourage Gold As a Rival to the Dollar?

The government knows all too well that given a choice, most Americans would prefer to hold silver and gold coins over dollars. They are not without their weapons against a real money status of gold and silver. They have crafted a way to keep you using paper bills and enforced this for decades now. This is through the use of the Federal tax code.

The IRS tax system in place discourages investors from owning gold and silver at all. They do this with a simple little capital gains tax rule on precious metals. If you own gold and silver and attempt to hold it as a hedge against declining paper dollar value, then they get you with a shockingly high 28% capital gains tax penalty when you move to sell it back into dollars.

To put this in simple terms, if you purchased five ounces of gold back when gold was at $300 per ounce in the early part of the last decade, and went to sell it back into dollars today at over $1,500 per ounce, then you would have to pay 28% of your $1,200 per ounce, or $6,000, gain. This means that of the $6,000 that you made, you would have to pay $1,680 of this in tax penalty.

If you do not think that the government is against your owning gold and silver, just consider the tax penalties on alternative investments. Stocks and bonds that you hold over a year are never taxed more than at 15% capital gains. Real Estate investments can qualify for even zero in taxes if you have a good accountant.

But if gold is treated as a currency like paper dollars, then there can be no tax rate applied to gains in gold and silver coins.

Suddenly, these coins would have as much as 28% more value to you as an investor or believer in the precious metals as real money. That would cause even more people to abandon their worthless paper dollars in favor of the precious metal coins.

Why is Gold as A Currency Bad News For The Feds?

Neither the Federal Reserve Bank nor the IRS want you to own gold and silver. When you do so, you sell your paper dollars in exchange for them. As this happens on a larger scale, it has dramatic ramifications for the government and its spending habits.

You see, the only way that the government has been able to pursue its runaway spending all of these years is through printing and borrowing money. They have drastically expanded the supply of dollars in the world by over 300% since 2007 alone.

If gold becomes a currency that finally puts the paper dollars out of business, then the Feds will lose their power to print money at will. They will no longer be able to inflate away their incredible fourteen trillion dollars in debts and to continue their reckless habits of over spending. They will have to learn to live within their means for a change.

Given the choice of using gold and silver money that never loses its value to a rising cost of living every year or of using paper dollars that arc less valuable every day, which would you choose?

Rescue Your Pension Funds From Government Seizing

You can not have missed the headlines that the U.S. has reached its borrowing limit of $14.3 trillion back in May.

This means that until and unless the debt ceiling is raised by Congress, the Federal Government officially has run out of enough money to fund all of its operations as of mid May.

So far they have found a way to juggle the books and keep all obligations met. Their solution presents a direct threat to your pensions, especially if you are a current or retired Federal employee.

In the paragraphs below, you will learn how the government is funding its operations, where they are getting the money from, how this could have serious consequences for your pension fund, and what you can do to protect your pension.

How Is the Government Funding Its Operations?

Once the Federal government reached its debt limit, or the amount of money that the government is able to borrow in order to finance its operations, they turned to creative accounting as a necessity. The Federal government brings in about half as many tax receipts as it needs to cover its costs each year.

The other approximately half is borrowed through the sale of Treasuries. The Treasury is also able to pick and choose what bills it pays and which ones it defers. This means that the government has some flexibility in paying its bills even when it can not borrow right now. So far, the Treasury Secretary Tim Geithner has been able to keep all of the bills paid. He says that he can continue to do so until August second.

Where is the Missing Money Coming From Until August Second?

Until the critical date of August second, the Treasury has found a source for the additional funds that they need to keep all of their operations going and all of their employees and debtors paid. The Treasury has begun to employ a number of adept maneuvers in order to cover all the bills.

They confidently announced that they will continue to meet all of their obligations until the second of August by halting all government investments in its two largest pension plans for employees of the Federal Government. Treasury discovered that it could come up with a total of $214 billion in additional funds through two ways.

The first is that they began to delay the substantial payments due to the Federal pension funds over the eleven weeks that lead up to August second. A much less well publicized second means of coming up with this money is in their withdrawing current investments that are already in the Federal pension funds.

They have reassured everyone that they will put the money back in the pension funds once they are able to have the national debt ceiling raised so that they can resume borrowing again.

But besides this Treasury move hat sets a dangerous precedent of them raiding your Federal pension funds next time they have a budget shortfall or run out of borrowing room, there is also no hard fast guarantee that they will be able to put the money back

How Much Does the Government Need to Borrow to Repay The Funds and Keep Operations Going?

For the Federal government to be able to put back the pension funds that they are both plundering and delaying, they will have to raise the debt ceiling first. There is much more at stake here than just your pension funds.

If the deeply divided Republican and Democratic congress is not able to find some compromise to their impasse on the fierce debate to raise the debt ceiling by the beginning of August, then the government will have no choice but to begin serious defaults on payments owed to some combination of employees, military personnel, contractors, or Treasury debt holders.

In order to keep the government running smoothly all the way through the beginning of 2013 and past the next national elections, they will require that the debt ceiling be increased by approximately $2.5 trillion.

What Other Consequences Could There Be Besides Pension Fund Depletion?

The consequences of Congress not coming to some agreement on the debt ceiling in time are far greater than the loss of your pension funds.

Federal Reserve Chairman Ben Bernake said in testimony in June that because of the amount of the Federal debt at over $14 trillion, and the uneven amounts of government revenue that come in every month, the juggling of books beyond this August second point could cause fear and even panic in the world financial markets.

The dollar's value would be significantly damaged, and the credit worthiness and ratings of the United States would be in serious doubt. These coveted national Triple AAA credit ratings could be downgraded by ratings agencies Moody's and S&P who have already threatened to lower the ratings if this impasse is not soon resolved. This would make it even more difficult for the Federal government to borrow the money that it needs to repay the Federal pension funds.

What Can You Do to Protect your Pension Plan Money?

If you are a member of the Federal Pension plans, the government already has its hand in your retirement pocket. You may be able to protect your funds by taking them away from the government if you act early. This is because with defined contribution pension plans, you are able to take early withdrawals of all or part of the money in many cases.

In order to learn if your pension plan will allow you to take the benefits out now, you would have to check with your pension plan documents or pension plan administrator. You can start by checking with your Summary Plan Description. This document details what your pension benefits are and the way that they are calculated.

There are rules on when you can request distributions of your benefits, so you should definitely consult with your plan administrator. Those of you who are in a defined pension benefit plan, or one that pays out a fixed benefit that is determined up front, are less likely to be able to take your money out of the pension plan. These types of plans often contain rules against taking money out early.

What Will Happen if you Withdraw Your Pension Benefits Now?

If you decide to save your pension plan money from government seizure, there are other consequences that you should be aware of when you withdraw your pension money. The IRS through your pension plan administrator will hit you with a ten percent penalty for early withdrawal of any funds.

On top of that, you will be assessed a standard twenty percent tax for the monies as well. This amounts to a steep thirty percent total penalty up front. Still, when you consider the possibility that you could lose potentially fifty percent or even all of your pension benefits if the government continues to overspend and gradually lose its ability to borrow money, these are better alternatives.

What do you think the chances are that the Federal Government will find a way out of its ongoing spending and debt mess in time to avoid seizing still more of your pension funds in the future?

<u>MONEY</u>

"Understanding the Medium of Exchange"

Money

The Five Deadly Consequences of Fiat Currencies

Although you may not be aware of what a fiat currency is, you actually use it every day. The U.S. dollar, as well as most major currencies in the world, are fiat currencies.

The paper bills, debit cards, and credit cards in your wallet all represent the fiat currency.

There are real problems with the economies of countries that use fiat currencies long term. In the following paragraphs, you will understand what a fiat currency really is, and what the five ruinous consequences of fiat currencies turn out to be.

What is a Fiat Currency?

Fiat money is actually money that does not have anything to back it up. It possesses purchasing power simply because the government says that it does through laws. In fact, the name originally comes from the Roman Empire days. In Latin, fiat stands for "let it be done." Such monies are thus created by government rule. Fiat money that government and citizens employ as a currency is referred to as fiat currency.

Even though there are numerous problems with fiat currencies historically, the shocking truth is that nearly every major reserve currency of the world is a fiat currency.

This includes the American dollar, the Eurozone Euro, the British Pound, and the Japanese Yen. It was the 1971 Nixon shock that started the move to current day fiat currencies when he and the other major economic powers of the world abandoned the gold standard.

A notable exception to this is Switzerland's Swiss Franc. While their currency is not officially on a gold standard anymore, it is still backed up by a gold reserve (that is mandated by their constitution) of twenty-five percent, with their gold valued at around $250 per ounce versus today's actual price of over $1,400 per ounce. This makes the Swiss Franc unique not only in that is backed up by gold, but also in that it is covered at a greater than one hundred percent gold value reserve.

What Are the Historical Problems with Fiat Currency?

Fiat Money has a long and distinguished history of failure. This failure goes back to the Roman Empire and continues all the way to today's Zimbabwe. The Romans devalued their Denarius coins from nearly one hundred percent pure silver down to only .02% by the fall of the empire.

The story is the same with the medieval Chinese empire of the 1100's with their "Flying Money," the French experiments with paper Livres, Assignats, and Francs over the centuries, and the Weimar Republic's worthless paper German Marks.

It is no exaggeration to say that each and every single fiat currency experiment in history has resulted in devaluation that led to final collapse of both the currency and the economy that utilized it. It is an ominous warning for us all today.

With this lesson of history in mind, consider the five deadly consequences that fiat currencies bring.

Lesson #1 - Fiat Currencies Cause Price Inflation

As revered economist Milton Friedman taught, inflation is always a phenomenon that is caused and driven by money. In other words, when too much money chases too few goods, prices rise in a vicious cycle. With every case of fiat money in history, including the U.S. dollar over the last forty years, governments who use paper money have inevitably decided to print extra money to help pay for things that they can not afford.

This causes prices of precious metals, commodities, food, and other necessities to rise. Consider the fact that the dollar has dropped around ninety-seven percent in value against gold since the U.S. dollar became a fiat currency not on the gold standard anymore. Prices of oil and gasoline have risen ten fold in the same time period.

Lesson #2 - Fiat Currencies Lead to Food Shortages

You see this food shortage phenomenon in the world today, especially in the Middle East. The continued use of fiat currencies around the globe and the over printing of the world's reserve currency the dollar especially aggravate this dire situation. The real problem is not that there is any true lack of food available.

It is instead that the price of food is being pushed up to unaffordable levels for many people in numerous countries.

This is a result of too much cheap fiat money that is flowing into food commodities such as wheat, corn, soybeans, and rice.

Many of these commodities have traded at long time highs both now and in the last few years as the crisis of fiat currencies has only grown worse. Sadly, you can expect this trend of high and rising food prices to only continue so long as fiat money rules the world.

Lesson #3 - Fiat Currencies Create Political Instability

The higher food prices that you see also cause political instability. None of these riots going on in the Middle East today began with a latent desire for democracy. Instead, they started as prices rose too high for the average working man to be able to provide for his family. A hungry person is a very dangerous one. The problems that are created as cheap fiat money floods the globe bring people out in the streets from Libya to Yemen.

Fiat currencies have also created political instability in Europe, the most sophisticated continent of all. You have seen this cause strikes, protests, and occasional violence in countries ranging from Greece and Ireland, to France and Great Britain. The severe austerity, or government spending cutbacks, measures that are being implemented in Europe are the result of the various European nations being forced to come back from the edge of ruinous spending that their fiat currencies made possible.

So long as nations are limited to what they can spend by a gold standard that backs up their currency, they can not run their financial houses into ruin.

With unlimited paper money, anything is possible for a while. Then the day of reckoning finally arrives and political instability results.

Lesson # 4 - Fiat Currencies Cause Speculative Booms and Busts

Because fiat currencies allow for money supplies to be expanded and contracted by central banks at will, they lead to speculative bubbles. Since the world departed from the gold standard forty years ago, there have been three speculative bubbles and a severe oil shock.

These boom and bust period that ranged from irrational exuberance in the overall stock market, technology stock arena, real estate prices, and sub prime mortgages all had one cause in common. Artificially cheap and overly available money caused these areas to inflate beyond reason.

Eventually, people catch on to the fragility of the bubbles, usually after someone blinks or an important event triggers collapse. Then the bust ensues, until the governments of the world are able to inflate yet another bubble when they make fiat money more readily available again.

Lesson # 5 - Fiat Currencies Make Wars More Prevalent

The Roman statesman and orator Cicero said it best when he opined that the sinews of war are unlimited money. Fiat currencies create the possibilities for limitless money to be created and spent. Governments with limitless supplies of cash are more likely to get into conflict with other nations around the world.

Paper money over the last forty years has made possible a large number of conflicts around the globe. This is true even as we are supposed to be living in a more civilized time when nations talk out their differences at the United Nations.

There are so many problems that fiat currencies have caused historically. Ironically, they are still causing these same problems today. Why do governments continue to try the old failed experiments with worthless paper money again and again and believe that the outcome will be any different this time around?

Without Additional Money Injection The Economy Will Crash

You have probably heard some of the talk about the imminent end of the Federal Reserve's much vaunted Quantitative Easing Two Program, more simply known as QE2. At the end of June, the Fed will cease and desist its second round of life support stimulus that the U.S. economy has enjoyed since the end of last year.

This is a momentous event for the overall economy that could have far reaching effects that even extend to your investment portfolio and strategy. In the paragraphs below, you will see what component of QE2 is actually ending, how the economy is responding to this conclusion, and what it will mean for interest rates and your investments going forward.

What are the Components of Quantitative Easing 2?

You should remember that there are two components to the second round of quantitative easing that the Federal Reserve provides. The most famous of these has been the six hundred billion dollars in money printing that the Fed has engaged in through buying Treasuries.

The idea behind this was to provide extra liquidity to the economy and to drive down interest rates, since they move inversely to the demand and price for these investments.

Lower treasury yields translate to lower interest rates throughout the economy, and this is supposed to trickle down to you, other consumers, and businesses and to encourage you to spend money that you obtain from cheap mortgages, car loans, and other forms of credit.

You should not overlook the other core component of QE2 that has been all but forgotten in the mix. The Fed Funds rate of zero percent, also known as the rate at which that the Fed loans money to banks, means that loans are already available to both you and businesses at historically low interest rates.

The goal of these two policies has been to jump start consumer spending, save the double dipping housing market, and hopefully indirectly encourage businesses to provide more jobs to ease the over nine percent unemployment rate.

How Well Has Quantitative Easing 2 Worked?

You are witnessing a fierce debate on the effectiveness of QE2 so far. Some analysts claim that it has saved the economy from a worse predicament than it would have been in without the support.

Others point to still shockingly poor home sales and prices, sky high unemployment, and mediocre gross domestic product growth, or the value of all goods and services produced in the country in a year, as signs that QE2 has only managed to push up stock values and commodity prices when banks and investors sought out places to park the almost free money that the Fed offered them.

How is the Economy Responding to the End of Quantitative Easing 2?

The fact of the matter is that the economy is not responding well to the end of June conclusion of the Treasury buying portion of QE2. True unemployment remains near multi-decade highs, housing prices are lower now than at the worst point of the Great Recession so far, and consumer confidence is in full blown decline along with the much lauded industrial production that has slowed dramatically. After a brief year of things looking like they were improving, economic indicators have turned sharply down with the promised end of the addicting QE2 stimulus.

Will the Fed Change Interest Rate Policy Soon?

Federal Reserve Chairman Ben Bernanke gave a grim assessment of the American economy June 7th in a speech and June 8th via the Fed's Beige Book release of data. He admitted that the growth in the economy is still "frustratingly slow." He then went on to say that the recovery has not really gained solid footing until you see greater results in job creation.

In light of his comments and the mounting evidence that the so called recovery has derailed, practically no one is betting that the Fed will raise the interest rates component of QE2 any time soon. The futures market prices in a twenty-five basis point rise in the interest rates by June of 2012.

If Interest Rates Stay the Same, What Will Happen?

If you go with the assumption that the Fed will not raise interest rates in August, then the easy money policies of QE2 will continue to a degree. Banks will still be able to borrow money cheaper than the interest rate returns that they can receive for holding treasuries.

Businesses and individuals will still be able to borrow money at historically low rates of interest. This does not mean that the economy will improve. In fact, with the expiring program of the money printing and Treasuries buying ending, the economy will likely manage to sputter along as it has lately at best.

This does not mean that the stock market will be hamstrung. Many analysts concur that the reason that the stock market has risen so far as it has in the last year has been because of the cheap and easy money provided by low interest rates as well as the Treasury bond buying program. Certainly stocks will not have the two jolts of adrenaline to count on with most of the QE2 program ending though.

What Does Raising Interest Rates Mean for Investing Tactics?

One day eventually, the Fed will be forced to raise interest rates in order to head off rising inflation, or the higher cost of goods and services, because of too much easy money chasing too few goods and services.

Whether this happens in August of this year or the middle of 2012, you can count on stocks finding higher interest rates to be significant head winds. At that point, you will want to be out of bonds as well, since when interest rates rise, bond prices fall.

Higher interest rates generally favor investments that benefit from better interest based returns, such as money markets and certificates of deposit. The dollar also usually rises as the U.S. interest rates are more competitive with those of other countries. Remember that the relationship between the dollar and stocks is often inverse. A higher dollar can mean lower stock prices.

Could The Fed Actually Announce a QE3 Program in August?

The real question in the minds of most investors now is will the Fed decide to pump up the economy with yet another dose of quantitative easing called QE3. Big Ben Bernanke did not promise anything in his speech, nor even allude to it. Still, there are a number of economists and pundits who feel confident that the Fed will be left without options except to push for more stimulus by the end of summer, particularly if the slide in housing prices and sales continues apace.

Unemployment and housing data are only two pillars of the economic framework. Stock prices are an important third one. Should these stock prices continue to decline as they have been so far in most of June with the end of QE2 on the horizon, then the pressure will be on for the government to pursue additional stimulus and economic life support. You can call this by any name that you like, but it will amount to a third round of quantitative easing.

What Might a QE3 Look Like?

Since the housing market remains the over arching theme in the scheme of economic problems, this is where the government will probably fire its next economic broadside. It remains to be seen what they will come up with exactly.

Whether they engage in a QE3 or not, so long as the interest rates stay low, money will be cheap for investors and banks to borrow and invest.

What do you think that the Fed means literally when it says that it will keep interest rates at the near zero percent levels of today for an extended period of time?

Bitcoin - A Virtual Currency Without Central Authority

As the confidence of people and governments around the world in the U.S. dollar has waned, some have pushed and called for another medium of exchange. You have seen states like Utah pass laws to allow gold and silver coins to be used along side the dollar.

You may not be aware of the fact that there is an alternative currency that you can utilize to pay for goods and services besides the dollar, gold and silver.

In fact, this new currency called Bitcoin is an all electronic means of payment that may one day change the whole face of international monetary transactions. In the paragraphs below, you will learn what Bitcoin is, how you can exchange them, what security issues are involved, and who is taking it very seriously.

What Is Bitcoin Exactly?

Bitcoin was created back in 2009 by Satoshi Nakamoto. It is the first international currency that is both virtual and decentralized. This new type of currency had no practical value only a few years ago. Since then it has grown to be more valuable than both the Euro and the US Dollar. In fact, a single Bitcoin today is worth around fifteen dollars.

Even though these Bitcoins have gained dramatically in value, this currency is not yet a true replacement for any other form of money in the world, such as the U.S. dollar, Euro, British Pound, or Swiss Franc. The easiest way to visualize it is as an electronic version of a commodity like silver or gold. With one ounce of silver or gold you are able to buy a certain number of dollars. With a Bitcoin, you can similarly purchase a variable quantity of dollars or Euros.

Why Has BitCoin Become So Popular?

Bitcoin has already appealed to a large audience for a number of reasons. The purpose of the currency strikes a cord with many users. It aims to give online participants almost the same anonymity as does cash. This cuts down on the possibility of identity theft over the Internet.

Bitcoin also can not be manipulated by governments who seek to print more money. This is because it is not issued by a government entity at all. Its supply is tightly controlled and strictly limited.

Besides this, Bitcoin does not involve banks, traces, or fees. If you are a person who likes your privacy and does not want your every financial transaction and activity monitored, then you can appreciate why this is so popular. You do not have to pay any costs to work with the Bitcoin currency either.

How is The Value of BitCoin Determined?

Since Bitcoin is not issued by or monitored by a central government authority and does not trade on the world Foreign Exchange, it does not have any entity to guide the currency value. Instead, the value comes from supply and demand, like with any commodity.

Bitcoin supply has been limited by the designer so that they will have a high value. They derive their demand from individuals who wish to have these Bitcoins to trade. This is to say that the value of Bitcoins can change significantly, since it is a new currency. Speculators in the currency can cause its value to rise or fall rapidly.

How Many Bitcoins Are There?

The number of Bitcoins is tightly controlled. There will not be more than twenty-one million of them created. They are only made when incredibly complicated math problems are solved. These math problems would take your home computer years to answer just a single one that would produce only one Bitcoin. This ensures that there will not be a flood of Bitcoins released to destabilize the new currency.

With so few of these coins in existence, you may wonder how they practically function. The answer lies in the fact that they can be sub-divided down to fully eight decimal places. So a good or service might cost .04 BTC's, the abbreviation for Bitcoins, or it could cost as little as .00000075 BTC's. As the value of the Bitcoins rises, the limited number that can be created may not seem so small anymore.

How Can You Exchange Bitcoins?

There is not only a single way that you can exchange bitcoins. The easiest way is to go the Internet and find out how much you will have to pay to obtain some BTC's. This can be expensive, based on the wide swings in their value and the availability of them at any given moment.

You can trade for Bitcoins as you do for dollars or Euros. This is a less expensive and extremely popular way to obtain these coins. When you offer a product, a service, or some information online, you can ask to be paid in Bitcoins. It may surprise you to learn that there are individuals and organizations now who request that you make donations in Bitcoins instead of through PayPal or dollar or euro based credit cards.

You might also buy and sell Bitcoins. Bitcoins have become popular enough that there are now exchange market places over the Internet that permit you to sell the BTC's for money. You can also arrange a private transaction to buy or sell Bitcoins through any arena that you choose.

There is another more complicated way to obtain Bitcoins, but it is impractical for most people. You could set up a large and powerful computer network that would solve the complex math problems that generate Bitcoins.

This is known as mining for Bitcoins, and it usually costs more than the value of the Bitcoins that you would obtain through it. You can also link up with joint ventures of people doing this, in what is called mining pools. Unless this is something that you are doing for fun, it does not usually turn out to be worth your while.

Where Are Your Bitcoins Kept and How Are They Protected?

When you download the Bitcoin program to get started, the default setting will be to put your Bitcoin wallet as a file located on your personal computer. This is the safest place to keep the wallet, but it is not fool proof, as with any wallet.

It can be stolen if you contract a computer virus or pick up other forms of eavesdropping malware. This stolen virtual wallet scenario is a problem that the Bitcoin developers are working to address.

Are Governments Taking Bitcoin Seriously?

Before you decide that the Bitcoin virtual currency is merely some online game or passing computer fad, you should know how seriously the U.S. government takes it. There has not been a truly global currency with which you could buy goods and services like this one attempted before now. Many individuals only see the new currency as a huge chance to make money when they participate in it in the early stages.

The CIA deems it enough of a potential threat to national security and a challenge to the dollar that they are looking into it. Gavin Andresen, the Bitcoin principal, will give a presentation to the CIA in June. The Central Intelligence Agency obviously takes this relatively new currency very seriously.

Does that not sound like a good reason for you to look into Bitcoin as well?

Money

<u>TOOLS</u>

"Instruments for Building a Wealth Foundation"

Wealth Trigger Review - Attract Success With Hypnosis

There are many different motivational products on the market to help teach you to think like a rich person. One of these is fairly unique in that it does more than simply give advice.

The Wealth Trigger by Joe Vitale and Steve Jones not only tells you what you need to learn in order to attract wealth, it actually uses hypnosis to retool your mind to be able to attract wealth.

In the following paragraphs, you will learn why this novel approach is an excellent way for you to get around your mental blocks that keep you from achievements in your life.

About the Authors Dr. Joe Vitale and Steve G. Jones

Dr. Joe Vitale has a long and interesting past in motivational speaking. For more than twenty years, he has demonstrated to people like you how to attract wealth and other types of success in life. The speaker has also authored more than fifty motivational books. You might have seen Vitale on his appearance on Larry King Live. He has also been in the blockbuster movie "The Secret."

Dr. Joe Vitale has teamed up with Steve G. Jones in order to bring you his Wealth Trigger product. This is because there is more than simply motivational speaking involved with the package. There is also hypnotherapy, something in which Steve Jones specializes.

Steve is a world famous hypnotist who works with celebrities and actors. He earned both a Master's Degrees in Cognitive Psychology as well as a Doctorate in Education that gave him an in depth background in the ways that people learn. He has written a number of bestselling books and practiced hypnosis for more than twenty-five years.

Among Steve's clients that he has helped over the years are actor Danny Bonaduce and screen writer of Superman the Movie Tom Mankiewicz. Steve has made feature appearance on NBC and TruTV.

What the Wealth Trigger Product Teaches You

This Wealth Trigger product teaches you many different concepts that will help you to be a success in all areas of your life. It starts out with the three components of the Law of Attraction. You must master these in order to harness the power of this law for your own benefit.

Closely connected to this is the necessary thought transformation. The product shows you the ways that you can change your negative thoughts into positive ones so that you can be a success in all of your endeavors.

The Wealth Trigger also shows you the secrets to job attraction and career attraction. One of the modules focuses on the precise steps that you need to follow in order to secure a new job that will help you to start earning money straight away.

Dr. Vitale goes beyond the necessary steps to find a job with his career attraction advice. He helps you to find the career that you really want and to quickly advance along the career path that you choose.

Another great segment that the Wealth Trigger features is the one on opportunity attraction. Since opportunities are all around you, it is a shame that you miss out on them all of the time. The product teaches you the ways to both recognize them and take advantage of them.

Use The Power of the Subconsciousness Mind

If you struggle to gain wealth as many individuals do, then the Wealth Trigger will show you how you are a victim of your sub-conscious mind. The sad truth is that your mind picks up little blocks to all types of success from when you are a baby all the way through adult hood.

In the end, as these are subliminal blocks, you are not even aware of them. This is to say that the subconscious mind can work against you as well as for you. With the Wealth Trigger, Dr. Joe Vitale and Steve Jones actually interact directly with your subconscious in order to remove these blocks.

They take out the negative ideas and replace them with positive ones that help you to attract wealth. This becomes your wealth trigger.

Why Hypnosis and Hypnotherapy Work

As you may already know, there are many products on the market that can tell you about the ways to attract wealth, jobs, and opportunities. What separates the Wealth Trigger from the competition is the novel approach to program this success in your subliminal mind. The authors do this through hypnosis and hypnotherapy.

It is easy to confuse the concepts of hypnosis and hypnotherapy, since they are interrelated. Hypnosis actually puts you into a deeply relaxed state so that the hypnotist can make suggestions to you that help to change your behaviors in your subliminal mind.

The reason that hypnosis works so well is because your body does not distinguish between an experience that you imagine and one that really happens. To your body, the physiological responses are identical, whether you go through the event itself or imagine that you go through it. This means that with hypnosis, your mind can be intellectually aware that a scenario has played out and respond to it like it really occurred, even though it did not actually happen.

Hypnotherapy carries this a step further. It combines hypnosis with therapy. This is what distinguishes it from the type of hypnosis that you watch a hypnotist perform at a show on stage. To affect hypnotherapy, the hypnotist mixes hypnosis with targeted therapy for your subconscious mind that focuses on exact outcomes and results.

This is quite different from the traditional forms of therapy with which you may be familiar. With traditional therapy, you have to spend greats amount of time with your therapist. This could even amount to years before you achieve real breakthroughs. Hypnotherapy is vastly different from this.

When you go through hypnotherapy like the types included in The Wealth Trigger modules, you reach your end goals in a rapid, effective, and dependable approach to change your negative behaviors. This hypnotherapy offers you the fastest reliable means to get the results of new beliefs and actions that you desperately need in order to attract wealth.

What Is Included with the Wealth Trigger Product?

The Wealth Trigger package includes ten different audio modules. The first four of them are motivational modules that Dr. Joe Vitale recorded to teach you all of the necessary ideas and steps that you need to internalize to attract wealth.

The next six modules are hypnotherapy sessions that Steve Jones hosts. Here he actually walks you through the necessary hypnosis exercises to reprogram your thought process so that you can attract wealth and success.

The package also includes an instructional book that has work book exercises. It is all the materials that you will need to get your mind on the right subliminal track to attain the wealth that has so far eluded you.

Is the Wealth Trigger a Good Value for the Price?

The cost is something that always raises suspicion and objection to self help packages like this one. The Wealth Trigger is not priced to be unaffordable. It can be had for as little as $39. Not only is the price reasonable, but it includes a risk free satisfaction.

If you are not convinced that the Wealth Trigger helped you after going through the modules and book, then you can get your money back for up to sixty days. At a low price and with such a reasonable guarantee, why would you not try out The Wealth Trigger product?

Investment Advice Review - The James Dines Newsletters

If you are interested in gaining better financial education to help you manage your investments, then you can read financial newsletters and study investment courses. While there are a number of these available, it is not easy to know which ones are the best.

James Dines puts out a newsletter that has been well respected for two generations now. His company also offers an investment alerts service and an investment course that will teach you what you need to know to effectively manage your own investments.

Who is James Dines?

James Dines is a long time investment adviser who has written his popular namesake newsletter since the 1960's. He has also authored five well respected books on investment and finance. Dines offers his videotaped master educational investment series. You can read the praises for his incredibly prescient investment ideas over the decades in Forbes, Barron's, Moneyline, the London Financial Times, and the New York Times to name a few.

This investment adviser has become legendary for his various correct calls that disagreed with the mainstream financial community time and again.

In his newsletter, he warned of an invisible crash in the stock market in 1966, the incredible and unforeseen boom in gold in 1974, the revolution of the Internet in 1996, and the Uranium boom in 2003.

Many of the subscribers to his newsletter that he has written since the 1960's and published independently since the 1970's have made so much money from The Dines' Letter that they hand their subscriptions down to second generations.

You have probably heard of technical analysis before, even if you are not so familiar with what it means. James Dines wrote the definitive instant classic on the subject aptly called "Technical Analysis" after a fourteen year labor of love. This book sells for a thousand dollars today in rare book stores.

Among Mr. Dines' great accomplishments is that he became the very first analyst on Wall Street to forecast that the dollar would experience an enormous devaluation. He predicted that this would happen once it was no longer backed by gold and silver. This prediction that he first made in the early 1970's continues to prove itself true even today.

James Dines' ability to predict the significant moves and turns in the stock market is impressive. He has correctly predicted these an astonishing nineteen out of twenty-one times. This represents a success rate that exceeds ninety percent.

What Does the Dines Letter Offer You?

The Dines' Letter has called gold and silver's meteoric rise, the rise of the Internet, the rise of China, and the importance of rare earth metals and uranium over the decades.

This flagship product is where the legendary analyst and author provides you with general market commentary on everything that is going on with stocks, bonds, silver, gold, uranium, rare earth metals, interest rates and other investment products.

With every issue, the author shares his thoughts on what the stock market is doing and where it is headed. He digs into current events and their impacts on investments. This goes far beyond politics and economics. Dines' investigates scientific discoveries, social events, health matters, and financial events as part of his tri weekly newsletter.

What is the Methodology of the Dines Letter?

James Dines employs a four part method for evaluating investments. Without all four keys, he claims that you can not achieve consistent investment success. His research starts with fundamental analysis, or the knowledge of the market or the company itself. He then uses the second key of technical or visual analysis that considers the trends of the prices of the stock and market. These two types of analysis are where many financial analysts stop.

Dines' analysis next considers mass psychology, the way that the psychology of other people in the masses will impact investments. Finally, it looks at the secrets of high states, or the ways that individuals' own personal attitudes and ideas impact investments.

It is the combination of all four keys in James Dines' own time tested and proven investment method that allows his letter to have such a huge number of major success over the years.

His use of all four keys has enabled him to call not only upcoming opportunities, but tops in these markets before they came back down.

What Does the Interim Warning Bulletin Offer You?

Many subscribers to the Dines' Letter are worried about what will happen to their investments in between the three newsletter issues per week. To answer the call for immediate updates on his recommendations, James Dines' began to offer the Interim Warning Bulletin Service.

This service is designed to help you watch over your portfolio as it makes you aware of important changes in the market in between issues on an urgent basis. It helps you to know when you need to execute major investment decisions at the critical moment that you must make them.

These bulletins are sent out by your choice of email or fax. Once an event that impacts markets occurs, you will learn about it. Such events could include a terrorist attack somewhere, a crisis in a foreign currency, or a fundamental or technical analysis warning that is issued. These are designed to help you make critical buy and sell decisions on a moment's notice.

For this service that only costs a dollar per day, you gain the peace of mind that both James Dines and his professional staff are on top of the market every trading day. They track the recommended investments and watch for signals in the market. They watch earnings' announcements and estimates for you. The service only sends out alerts as they have something important to tell you.

What is the Master Course Investment Strategy Method?

Dines has also put together a master video course on investment strategy. This all inclusive guide for how to make money in the challenging next few years eliminates the need for you to have to spend the significant time and money that you would at investment seminars. It is designed to teach you the methods to build up your own intelligent and safe investment portfolio not only for today, but for the future.

The series is comprised of four videos. Dines goes through the reasons that explain why the world is in so much trouble today. He walks you through events that could trigger another rapid stock market decline. The series then explains to you what you should do to protect yourself and profit.

Dines shows you that there are investments that are lucrative and still safe to own in the ongoing crash. He teaches you which investments these are and shows you tangible proofs for why they will increase in value.

Dines also demonstrates to you the things that you need to do before and after the next stage of the financial crash occurs. The goal is to help you learn how to not only safeguard your investment capital, but to achieve high returns in the process.

If you are in search of good financial education, you should certainly investigate all that James Dines has to offer. He can teach you how to invest for yourself, make you aware of upcoming trends in the markets, and keep you up to date on the daily factors that affect his recommendations. How can you argue with his five decade track record?

The Secrets And Dirty Tricks of High Frequency Trading

When you think of stocks, bonds, and other investments, you are probably familiar with the old buy and hold strategy that financial advisers and stock brokers have recommended for decades. This is the strategy that a great number of individuals follow with their own portfolio and investments.

There is another form of investment trading that you may not have heard much about, called High Frequency Trading. This High Frequency Trading has grown more and more significant in the last few years. You now see it impacting the holdings of average and ordinary investors like yourself.

The paragraphs that follow explain what High Frequency Trading is and reveal some of the secrets and dirty tricks that it plays on the markets.

What is High Frequency Trading and Why Does It Matter?

High Frequency Trading is actually an easy concept in theory. If you are involved in the practice, then you buy and sell a huge number of positions in stocks, exchange traded funds, futures, options, currencies, and other investments on an every day basis.

Your goal with this form of trading is to make small amounts of per unit profits on positions that you may only take and hold for even a few minutes. High Frequency Trading usually involves you trying to find anomalies in the prices of stocks or other investments that may only last for a few seconds, minutes, or sometimes hours.

You will find that the practice of High Frequency Trading is more involved and complex than the theory. First of all, for this form of trading to be successful, it must be executed very quickly. It also requires a great deal of turnover in investment positions, since the goal is to make even fractions of a penny or a few pennies on any trade.

Most high frequency traders will enter and exit numerous positions in less than a day. The majority of firms that engage in the trade do not hold their positions overnight, so they eliminate the risk of events that might move the markets in between trading sessions. Most of this type of trading does not use protective stop positions to limit losses, since if you are a high frequency trader, you are prepared to exit a position quickly anyway.

Why is this important to you as a more traditional buy and hold investor or even someone who trades in and out of positions on a more frequent basis? In 2010, this High Frequency Trading had become such a huge part of the stock markets within the United States that more than seventy percent of all stock equity trades were considered to be high frequency, according to estimates from the TABB Group.

The same company believes that high frequency trade profits could amount to around eight billion dollars every year. This style of trading does not only impact U.S. investors.

It gains in popularity and volume every year in both Asian and European markets as well. Because of this, the impacts that it has on the markets and potentially your investments are huge.

How does High Frequency Trading Work?

High Frequency Trading is too fast for you to do without significant help. The amount of time that is required for you as an individual to analyze huge amounts of information on a number of different securities makes it practically impossible to perform unaided. This is why firms that do this style of trading use high speed computers and algorithms.

The super computers are to look at information rapidly and making instant decision. Hundreds of algorithms, or complicated mathematical computations that are programmed in to these computers, work to find the trades. The computers even make most of the trades while the people who watch over them keep an eye on the process. For example, the computer algorithms might be set up to look for arbitrage, or brief imbalances between prices on one or more stocks or other investments.

When they locate such an imbalance in price, these programs will enter the trade, look for the momentary price move, and then exit it all automatically. To do this, you must have the capability to analyze everything that happens in the market literally as it occurs.

What are the Requirements of High Frequency Trading?

High Frequency Trading most always involves high start up and ongoing costs. Most High Frequency Traders use their own money for the trades.

This means that they will require a significant amount of trading capital to execute large positions. You already have seen that expensive high powered computers are necessary.

These computer algorithms are even more costly, since any serious High Frequency Trader will not simply use the same hundreds of programs again and again. In order for the programs to be successful, they have to be changed every four to six weeks at the latest. This translates to programming expenses of millions of dollars in order to have programmers create a hundred different varieties of the same algorithm or group of algorithms.

Who is Engaged in High Frequency Trading?

By now you understand that the individual investor can not afford to become a high frequency trader unless he is a part of a larger organization. There are three types of companies that engage in this form of trading.

Broker-dealers are the outfits that trade stocks for individual investors. There are somewhere between ten and twenty of these companies that have their own trading desks that engage in high frequency trades on their own behalf. A second group that pursues this are the High Frequency Hedge Funds.

These less than twenty in number trading outfits use their own members private money. The most common High Frequency Trading category is represented by the independent outfits that number somewhere between one hundred and three hundred.

What are the Effects on the Market and on a Single Stock?

You can see that there are mixed effects that this High Frequency Trading produces on the market. The positive ones include an enormous improvement in the liquidity of the overall market. With seventy percent of all trades now estimated to be of these type, the stock market volume is far greater as a result of it.

Advocates of this type of trading also point to lower trading costs that result from this greater volume. The markets are also better linked as a result of it, and the stock and other security quotes are more detailed and up to the minute.

The problem that you have is that most of these benefits only appear in calm markets. In markets that begin to decline, High Frequency Trading has actually wreaked havoc. This is because these types of traders immediately sell their positions and then disappear from the market when it turns too volatile.

Suddenly more than two thirds of stock market volume disappears at once. The results can be catastrophic as most of the buyers are all gone. What might be a hundred or two hundred point decline can suddenly turn into a nightmarish crash of over five hundred points. The May 6, 2010 Flash Crash of over nine hundred points in a matter of minutes is the best example of this.

With what you now know about High Frequency Trading, are you surprised that it was discovered to be one of the main culprits in this second largest intra-day stock market decline in history?

<u>WEALTH</u>

"Pursuing Prosperity with Financial Education"

The 6 Golden Rules To Retire Financially Independent

In the 6 Golden Rules of Building Wealth, the author Roberto Lanzillotti offers the secrets to getting rich. More than this, he lays out a very practical and clear guide for the ways to retire early and retire financially independent.

You will find the e-book a refreshing take on the meaning of financial wealth and independence. For example, Lanzillotti says that financial freedom is defined as the ability for you to maintain your determined standard of living and not need to work any more.

To do this, the author goes against conventional wisdom when he tells you that you will not be able to count on investments in managed funds, a job that pays well, trading foreign exchange or stocks, or a business that you have to be present at all of the time. In the e-book, you will find six golden rules to effectively become wealthy.

Rule #1 - Use Passive Income to Build Wealth

The 6 Golden Rules of Building Wealth is quick to point out that wealth does not equal money. Instead, it says that it is about free time.

The only way that you are able to create free time is through boosting your income while lowering the number of hours that you put in at work. This is done when you put your money to work on your behalf. It is accomplished through passive income, which the wealthy all employ.

How do you set up passive income for yourself? Lanzillotti tells you that it is done when you acquire assets. Assets are a concept that is often confused. Assets are things that put money in your bank account. The greater number of these that you possess, the greater amount of passive income that you are able to generate. The best income producing assets that you should look tog gain are real estate, dividend yielding stocks, franchises or businesses that can be run absentee, and royalties.

Rule #2 - Take Control

One thing that author Lanzillotti makes a point of is that it is not a financial manager or expert's job to make certain that you can afford to retire comfortably and securely. Such individuals work for companies whose goal is to make money, not to ensure your retirement. They get paid regardless of their performance on your behalf.

The majority of retirement strategies are rooted in the growth of capital. The problem with this is that you need to take control of your income away from the factors that affect capital growth. This is because capital growth in such investments as stocks is based on the emotions of many people that you are unable to control.

You can learn about investments that you are actually able to control through education. You have to make it a point to become financially literate.

You might do this through going to seminars, reading books on financial education and success stories, and by interacting with financial mentors.

After you learn about wealth creation, you will finally have to apply this knowledge. This way, you will be able to develop your own particular strategy. There is nothing to prevent you from engaging the services of experts such as accountants, stock brokers, and bankers along your way. The key is that they follow your instructions, so that you are in control of the entire wealth generating process.

Rule #3 - Focus, Focus, Focus

Many people fall into a trap when they make too many big goals. Instead, you should focus on fewer, more specific goals. They should be achievable, specific, and also a challenge. You should not scatter shoot your efforts from one goal to another either. If you wish to become rich, then you should concentrate your efforts to create not active income, but passive income instead. People who are successes concentrate all of their energies on only one task until it is done. This gets far superior results.

The e-book recommends that you first determine how much money that you need for your early retirement. It is true that wealth is relative. What one person needs to support himself will be different from the next person. You need to know the amount of money that you would require to keep up your standard of living if you were going to retire today.

Once you have learned this, you can determine the way that you wish to make money. There are three basic means to do this. You can work for money on a job.

You can work for yourself in a business. Or you can work smarter and not harder to generate money through passive income. To create passive income as an investor, you have to learn how to save, trade, and invest. The saving part is self explanatory. Traders must learn how to appraise assets and understand the appropriate time to purchase and dispose of them. Investors have to comprehend the means to properly manage assets, cash flow, and risks over the long haul.

Rule #4 - Use Leverage

The definition of leverage is to accomplish more while you make a smaller effort. Leverage is among the most potent means that you can use to make success and build wealth. You should employ more types of leverage as you progress.

This means that you should work through other people's efforts, move on good ideas, build up a network, gain financial education, and work with your extra time to create a passive income business or to invest in real estate or stocks that yield dividends.

You should also employ financial leverage wherever and whenever you can. Remember that while average people attempt to grow wealth with their own money, rich people utilize other groups' money in order to create wealth. Financial leverage means that you employ good debt to get ahead financially. Good debt makes you money, while bad will take money away from you.

Learn more about the power of leverage in The Wealthy Code written by George Antone.

Rule #5 - Build a Surplus

Lanzillotti the author also instructs you to build up a cash surplus in order to achieve wealth. You will have to set up some financial statements in order to see if you have more cash that comes in every month than goes out of your accounts. You can set up a balance sheet and personal income statement to achieve this. Income statements break down your expenses and income.

It demonstrates what your actual net cash flow position is, whether it is a shortfall or a surplus. Balance sheets show your financial status at any given point. They demonstrate where your money is working, or assets, and the means and costs of the capital that you have acquired, or liabilities. This will reveal to you your actual net worth.

The formula for net worth is simply stated as your total assets minus your total liabilities. To build up wealth effectively, you must properly manage your cash flow so that more money comes in than goes out. With the surplus, you can buy assets that give you passive income.

Rule #6 - Follow Your Life's Purpose

The sad thing is that the majority of people muddle through their lives without comprehending their purpose. There are two ways that you can approach life. You might do what most people do and follow the plan that society lays out. If you do this, then you will have a life marked by stress, fear, worry, and bitter regret. You will stagnate and ignore your abilities and talents.

Alternatively, you might learn what the purpose of your life is and follow those dreams. The passion and energy that this creates in your life will inspire you.

The saying do what you love and the money will follow is so true. Wealthy individuals are not about going after money so much as they are about going after their dreams. Ask yourself this: how can I make money doing what I love and enjoy?

Where Do I Get This Ebook?

This ebook is available in our member area. If you are not a member yet please sign up for our Wealth Building Course.

Five Top Financial Education Books to Build Your Wealth

You may be aware that there are countless financial advice books available on the market today. As you might expect, some of them are better and more useful for you than others are. Five financial education books are especially helpful in your quest to understand how to grow and protect your wealth.

In the paragraphs that follow, you will learn what they are, as well as the practical lessons that you can learn when you put in the time and effort to read these excellent financial guide books.

1. The Cashflow Quadrant - Rich Dad, Poor Dad

Rich Dad, Poor Dad is financial writer and speaker Robert Kiyosaki's first and most successful self help book on finance. He sets up this interesting read in parable style to go through good and bad lessons that the author learned from two men in his life as he grew up.

It teaches financial independence that you can achieve when you acquire businesses, real estate, and investments. The book also advocates techniques that you can use to protect your investments and assets. This work is the best selling self help personal financial book of all time. This makes it well worth you reading it all by itself.

You should also read it because it teaches you about the differences between assets and liabilities. You may confuse the two as do many Americans. The book also shows you what the cash flow quadrant means and how and why you must understand and master the ideas behind it.

When you learn about the four ways that you can make money, as an employee, self employed, business owner, and investor, then you will come to understand why you will make far more money as a business owner or investor than as an employee or self employed individual. The book will also show you how to generate and acquire high yield assets to greatly expand your wealth.

2. Fiat Currency - The Web of Debt

Ellen Brown wrote a masterful translation of the complicated subject that surrounds current day money and how the government creates it in her book "The Web of Debt." Brown removes the cloak of mystery that surrounds fiat currency money that you use today.

You may not know that the government creates all money today through loans that private banks and the Federal Reserve advance to businesses and people. In order for them to make interest, they have to constantly loan out new money, which both boosts the money supply and inflates prices.

Web of Debt teaches you not only the history and evolution of how money got to this point, it shows you why you need to grow it faster than the inflation rate so that your savings and investments do not lose value.

Besides this, it gives solutions and alternatives for a better system of money than one that is based on a banking system that requires banks to make profits in order for it to work. It is imperative that you understand how fragile the money system really is in this country so that you can protect your wealth and assets.

3. Economic Cycles - Guide to Investing in Gold and Silver

Another book that you should read is Michael Maloney's "Guide to Investing in Gold and Silver." This book makes its mark as the primer for everything that you need to understand concerning the relationships between precious metals and money.

It shows you what the actual economic cycles are that cause both gold and silver to be the true standards for money. The book demonstrates how the American government actually creates inflation when they print more money and thereby weaken your money's value.

The book does more than this. In practical application, it makes the case for why investments in precious metals are actually among the soundest, simplest, and potentially most profitable ones that you can make.

It goes a step further as it shows you how, where, and when you should invest your money in order to achieve the greatest possible returns, regardless of how the economy performs. "Guide to Investing in Gold and Silver" caps it off as it provides you with critical advice on how to eliminate the middle man so that you can gain personal control over your own investments and finances.

4. Leverage - The Wealthy Code

George Antone wrote a terrific work to help you understand the secrets to grow wealthy in "The Wealthy Code." He uses the format of a story that involves an extremely rich man who confides his practical secrets in the main character in the book.

It teaches you the pertinent details of this code that they rich use to grow their money. As it does so, it imparts the ideas of what wealth is, how you create it, and how you evolve into a rich person. The book features powerful concepts that you really need to master. The idea behind leverage turns out to be among its best secrets. You must learn to use the money of other people in order to attain wealth.

This is the difference between good and bad debt. Good debt allows you to bring in money to your accounts, while bad debt takes it away from you regularly. Once you master this powerful concept and multiply your money, you will be able to control a much greater base of assets that produce income for you. This will put you on the path to achieve true wealth.

5. The Inner Game - Secrets of the Millionaire Mind

The last of the five great wealth education books that you need to read and learn lessons from is the "Secrets of the Millionaire Mind," by Harv Eker. The author is a multimillionaire who sets out to show you the attitudes that you must have to become wealthy. He says that you must start with positive thoughts that will direct you on to positive actions. Such actions will give you good results.

Wealthy people start with an underlying attitude. They believe that they can succeed, and so they learn to succeed. There are seventeen principals that the book teaches.

Among them you will learn how and why wealthy individuals understand that they determine their own life even when poor people feel like they are powerless victims in life.

The wealthy look for opportunities where poor people only see obstacles to success. Fear does not stop the wealthy individuals, but it does hinder the poor. Rich people always seek to learn something new and grow as a person, while the poor are confident that they already know everything that is worth learning. Perhaps the greatest lesson from the "Secrets of the Millionaire Mind" is that you must learn how important it is to pay yourself first.

If you simply wait until you have paid all of your bills and expenses, then you will find that there is nothing left to save at the end of the month. This is because your expenses will always expand to soak up money left in your account. When you pay yourself first, the money will not lie around for you to fritter away.

These are only the highlights from the above five works. Can you imagine how much progress that you can make towards true wealth just by following the lessons that these five best wealth education books teach?

Hyperinflation in America Seminar Review - Lira Gonzalo

If you turn on the financial channels or watch them online, you will hear commentators and guests discuss the prospects for severe and runaway inflation in the states in the near to medium term future.

There is a growing chorus of economists who are worried about this scenario. Some of them say it could come as early as 2011.

There is now a video training seminar available to you online that educates you all about this prospect of high and runaway inflation, called "Hyperinflation in America." You will read about this product and the solutions that it offers in the following paragraphs.

About the Author Gonzalo Lira

The author of this Hyperinflation in America package is Gonzalo Lira. He is an American born person with family and roots in Chile. As such, Gonzalo Lira is well acquainted with Chile's own experience with hyperinflation that very personally affected his family. Lira has made an interesting and varied career as a novel writer, filmmaker, and finally economic blogger.

Since 2010, he has worked as a contributing economic analyst to a variety of well followed economic sites such as Business Insider, Seeking Alpha, Zero Hedge, and Naked Capitalism.

He also publishes his own eponymous blog that happens to be the tenth most heavily followed and visited economic blog on the Internet.

How Is Hyperinflation Defined?

"Hyperinflation in America" points out that hyperinflation is vastly different from plain old inflation. Inflation is comprised of prices that rise at a manageable level of several percent per year. Some economists argue that a small amount of inflation is a sign that an economy is healthy and is growing at full capacity.

Gonzalo Lira says that when inflation approaches and then exceeds twenty percent unchecked, then the tipping point is reached and hyperinflation takes hold. Hyperinflation means that banks, companies, and individuals have lost faith in the currency. The author tells you that it is in essence a loss of confidence in the currency of a country. This leads to shocking price increases that can be in the hundreds and thousands of percents in small amounts of time.

What Will Cause Hyperinflation in America?

The sad truth is that the majority of American investors and consumers are totally unaware that they will soon go through a terrible and deep economic crisis on a grand scale. Such a hyperinflation shock will not be unique to the United States; it has occurred in numerous nations at various times. Weimar Republic Germany, South and Central America, Eastern Europe, and most recently Zimbabwe have all suffered from hyperinflation.

You probably wonder what could cause such a phenomenon in the United States. Lira tells you that it is already in the works. The United States government's loose fiscal policies and bailouts, coupled with the cheap money agenda that the Federal Reserve has pursued, will insure that it begins. Prices will rise as a result of the flood of overly available U.S. dollars on the market.

What will turn high inflation into hyperinflation is when the people lose their faith in the depreciating currency and start to trade all of their paper and electronic dollars for commodities and food. This turns into a self perpetuating and vicious cycle when individuals are forced to sell their assets and dollar holdings in order to buy essential items like food, gas, and clothing.

Why Won't The Government Contain Inflation as it Did in the Early 1980's?

Lira very astutely points out some limitations of the Fed's inability to contain inflation and head off hyperinflation today. The American central bank was able to do this in the early 1980's under then Fed Chairman Paul Volcker when it raised interest rates to over eighteen percent.

The problem with this strategy now is that the government's debts have grown so large at over fourteen trillion. If the Fed tried to raise rates now, then the interest charges on the debt alone would bankrupt the government. This means that they will not use the only method that they have at their disposal to contain runaway inflation.

How is the Hyperinflation in America Training Video Broken Down?

Gonazlo Lira breaks down this interesting and informative video product into four segments. In the first segment, he discusses the tell tale signs that hyperinflation is already beginning to rear its ugly head in the American economy. He tells you the point where regular inflation turns into hyperinflation, past the breaking point of twenty percent a year. He also explains the unsettling ways that crises caused by hyperinflation typically end, in dictatorship.

In the second segment, the video warns against suckers' investments in survivalist gear and beliefs that American society will completely break down as hyperinflation arrives. The product focuses on real dangers, like the collapse in value of IRA's and 401K's that could even be seized by the U.S. government and converted into then worthless Treasury bonds. Here, Lira also begins to talk about the way that he would invest ten thousand dollars right now in order to make money during the imminent collapse of the U.S. dollar.

Segment three goes into details on how to use asset protection strategies in countries like Switzerland to safeguard your physical assets. It also talks about home mortgages and the way that you should use them against the hyperinflation scenario. In this segment, Lira shares an incredible investment opportunity that his uncle passed on when Chile suffered through hyperinflation.

The final segment goes into detail on the kinds of assets that Gonzalo Lira suggests that you should buy now and sell later at the lowest point of the collapse in the U.S. dollar. He warns you about four kinds of companies that you should not invest in when hyperinflation is happening.

He tells you the points to exit your hyperinflation trades as you see certain signals that the crisis is ending. The segment finishes with strategies for your to invest when these signals begin.

Suggestions on How to Protect Yourself And Your Investment

You should know that "Hyperinflation in America" provides hope for those who are prepared. If you follow its advice, then you will do more than just get through the coming hyperinflation, you will greatly prosper. Gonzalo Lira warns that you will not do this with traditional investments like stocks, bonds, or even real estate. Even if their own values do not decline, they will lose value with the declining value of the dollar.

Lira instead suggests that you buy commodities using debt as the smartest way to utilize your assets before hyperinflation breaks out. This is because commodities will increase significantly in price as they are a store of value. Debt will decrease in value along with the currency. You will be able to sell your commodities little by little to service the debt even as it declines in value.

The good news offered by the product is that hyperinflation will end. It always does, since people require a stable currency as a medium of exchange. You have to be prepared for the reality after hyperinflation is over.

When the end of hyperinflation finally arrives, Lira would have you sell your commodities and precious metals. He would have you take the enormous proceeds to buy back into desperately undervalued stocks and real estate.

The idea is that these investments that you purchase at rock bottom prices will then come back. You would then make another fortune on the rebound. Does this not sound like a better strategy than to simply buy non perishable foods and hope for the best?

The Most Effective Ways to Build Up Wealth In Your Life

If you are like the majority of people, then you do not have a large trust fund that waits for you or a big cash settlement from a lawsuit to help you meet your financial goals and to retire. For you to obtain wealth, you will have to achieve it on your own.

This is what is meant by the phrase to pull yourself up by your bootstraps. But while you probably agree with this assessment of your own financial prospects, you likely do not know how it is that you can grow wealthy.

There are some financial secrets that may seem somewhat obvious once you hear them. Pay attention to these so that you can learn the most effective ways to build up wealth in your own life.

Wealth is Usually Built Up Slowly

This may be frustrating to hear, but wealth is not usually built up quickly. Instead, it is achieved when you carefully and deliberately make a plan, adjust it as circumstances dictate, and then work hard to follow through with it. You are only deluding yourself if you think that you will suddenly achieve wealth in a lottery like fashion.

The first secret that you have to internalize is that you will probably spend many years in the quest to build up wealth and become wealthy. It may even take you until you approach retirement age. The important thing is that you are on the right path and that you take steps to reach your goal every day. Until you start the journey towards this destination, you will certainly not arrive there.

Wealth is Achieved Through A Simple Formula

For the vast majority of people like you, wealth is reached when you follow a simple and not too flashy formula. This is that wealth equals savings plus investment. In other words, there are two components that you must work on in your quest to achieve wealth.

Saving is a time honored concept that has mostly become a lost art in the United States in the past few decades. Until the Great Recession and Financial Crisis changed everything about people's attitudes towards savings, the personal savings rate in the U.S. stood at from about zero to negative numbers.

It has increased to more than five percent in the wake of the failures of banks, major unemployment, and credit line reductions that you have seen close to you or personally experienced. Still, the savings rate in this country is the lowest in the industrial, developed world. Consider that in France and Germany, it is over ten percent.

Financial experts suggest that you should save ten percent of your income.

Retirement planners will tell you that you need to put aside fifteen percent of your earnings if you wish to reach a somewhat reasonable level of replacing half of your working income when you arrive at the age to retire or at least to work less hours. If you want to achieve real wealth, you may need to save even more than this amount.

You Must Begin to Invest In Order to Achieve Real Wealth

The second part of the equation is perhaps the most important one. While you must save money in order to have money to invest, you will most likely never get ahead if you simply sock away your money in your mattress or in a low interest account that serves to barely keep your money ahead of the annual rate of inflation.

Instead, you have to look for investments opportunities that can appreciably grow your money. There are many of them out there, but some of them are better than others. To learn which ones are the most appropriate places for your money, you should begin to educate yourself financially.

All of the Wealthy Build Up a Financial Education

One thing that the rich practically all have in common is that they take the time to learn about how to grow their money. The school system certainly does not teach this. There are many ways to educate yourself financially. You can take some classes on finance and investment at your local community college or university.

This will take some time and money, but it is a wise way to spend both. You can also educate yourself through reading good books for personal finance and investing. A good one to start with is Robert Kiyosaki's "Rich Dad, Poor Dad" series.

This is an excellent entry level book that will start to give you some background on and comprehension of sensible techniques in investing.

If you read one financial or investing book a month, you would be amazed at how much you would know and understand about money management and investing at the end of the year. Newspaper and magazine articles will help to keep you on the cutting edge of what is happening with the investment world.

You can also attend seminars and workshops on investing your money wisely. There are many of these that guest speakers offer around the country. There will be some cost involved, but you can learn a lot in only a single day or two through such events. You should never stop learning about and listening to ways to manage your money.

The Rich Put Money To Work For Them

The saying that the rich do not work for money, they make money work for them is very true. They do this through a concept called passive income. Passive income is a means of generating money that you do not directly work for with your time and skills.

It involves building up some form or stream of income that will continue to provide you with regular and periodic cash flow. Cash flow investments like these are critical if you are going to build up sustainable wealth.

There are countless examples of passive income and cash flow investments that you can pursue. The most popular one these days is to establish an Internet based business. This might involve you starting up a blog and gathering up advertisers to bring in money.

You might also create some form or e-commerce store to sell products, information, or ideas. Passive income and cash flow investments like these can take some time to build up, but they will provide you with an additional stream of revenue that you need to achieve wealth more rapidly.

Many kinds of investments are also considered passive income or cash flow types. If you buy a rental property house and rent it out, the income that this produces is passive and yields helpful cash flow. You can also put your money into mutual funds, investment funds, and stocks that pay high dividends. These will provide you with monthly or quarterly checks that help to supplement your income and aid you on your way to growing wealthy.

The Rich Know Where the Back Door Is Located

This last point may amuse you, but it is so true. One thing that separates the wealthy from you and the rest of Americans is that they always know where they back door is in any establishment that they find themselves. This is to say that they always have a back up or alternate plan ready in case their first one does not work out. Have you considered where the back door is in your own financial situation and plan lately?

The 12 Principles of Building Wealth And Financial Freedom

What sensible person would not be interested to learn the secrets to increase wealth and achieve an early retirement? This may sound like a far fetched notion to you today in light of the dismal economy.

Actually, I strongly believe that the current economic problems are also a result of not understanding what wealth is, and the principles of building it. Too much focus these days is on money, which is only a derivative of wealth.

The truth is that you can reach these enviable goals if you follow twelve basic principles. These twelve principals are outlined and described for you in the paragraphs that follow.

1. Study the History of Money

There is more to know about the history of money than you might suppose. When you study about money and its historical norm, then you will understand the dangers that today's fiat money poses to your investments, retirement accounts, and other savings.

You have to know that the government employs fiat money to intentionally and steadily debase, or devalue, money by stealth. This is so that modern day sovereign governments can constantly spend more money every year and grow their debt little by little.

They then inflate away the value of their debt as they quietly print more and more money over time. You the saver and investor are one of the losers in this equation, unless you learn the ways to fight the ongoing stealth devaluation.

2. Understand the Cycles And New Rules of Money

There are many things that have changed about money in today's economy and world. You must understand these in order to grow your wealth. For instance, not all debt is bad. Some forms of debt leverage can allow you to create passive income investments that generate cash flow and give you additional net income on a regular basis.

Whenever interest rates are changing from low to high or high to low the economy functions on new rules. These periods are also called wealth cycles.

In 1971, the world experienced one of the largest global financial shift it had ever known. President Nixon removed the U.S. from the gold standard and with that single, seemingly insignificant act, the American dream ended for most of us. The dollar is no longer real, value-based money; it has become worthless currency and it's value is headed toward zero!

Savers and employees are now the losers, debtors and entrepreneurs the big winners.

3. Know the Difference between Money and Wealth

This may come as a shock to you, but money does not equal wealth. Wealth is the financial means to not have to work, or to pursue the activities that are of interest to you personally with your time.

Wealth is defined in the dictionary as: An abundance of valuable material possessions or resources; riches, the state of being rich; affluence, all goods and resources having value in terms of exchange or use, and a great amount; a profusion. It is also interesting to mention that health and wealth are closely related to each other.

Naturally, this means that the exact definition of wealth is different from you to the next individual. Until you comprehend the difference between money and wealth, you will not set your goals for reaching retirement early with the maximum effectiveness.

4. Leave the Past Behind You

Maybe you have made a mess of your financial situation in the past. Perhaps you are half way to the retirement age and you do not have much of anything, or even anything at all, saved for the golden years. It is time to forget about your past. Stop letting it control you.

Instead, pour all of your time, effort, and energies into what you can do to improve your financial condition in the present day. When you squander your days mulling over the bitter past, you only cheat yourself out of the more promising future that could await you with some hard work and prudent financial planning.

Your attention is one of the most valuable assets you have. Your attention span is limited and if you have attention fixed on the past you have less available to create and manifest your future. Wealth building is a long term commitment that goes far beyond your lifespan.

The poor prepare for Saturday evening, the middle class prepare for retirement and the wealthy prepare for generations to come.

5. Tap Into the Wealth Mindset

The biggest difference between the wealthy and everyone else is their outlook on life and their attitude. Poor people tend to be pessimistic. Middle class individuals are often realists by nature. The wealthy instead are optimists in every area of their life.

They realize that each day presents them with a golden opportunity to improve their financial lot in life. You can draw on the considerable source of power that this offers the rich too, whatever your present day financial circumstances may actually be.

A wealthy mind is focused on solving problems and working towards a solution. The wealthy mind is also interested in serving and improving the life of others.

6. Research Ways That Create Money

Did you know that there are smarter, more effective ways to create more money than only by working? You can look into effective avenues to set up passive income streams. This might involve you starting to develop an online business, an e-commerce website, or to invest in high yield dividend stocks with your portfolio.

When you put some time into this research task, your rewards can be far greater than whatever time, funds, and energy you expend to learn these secret ways to have more money every month.

We have left the industrial age, and are now in the information age. With this paradigm shift comes new rules. The traditional employment structure is vanishing and replaced with more entrepreneurs. The Internet is one of the new platforms of doing business, which is completely independent from the physical world.

7. Learn How to Protect Your Money

Risk management is a fancy way of saying that you should protect your money and not gamble it away in a risk fraught investment casino. There are effective strategies to protect your stock portfolio and other investments.

Insurance on many forms of investments is both available and a prudent choice for you. But you will not even know that this financial insurance is available to you for a reasonable premium if you do not spend some time to learn how you can protect your money.

8. Understand How to Budget Your Money

It may come as a surprise to you to learn that many people do not even have a monthly budget off of which they work and operate. Over half of American households fall into this category. Until you learn how to budget your resources so that there can be money put aside with which to save and invest, you will never get ahead financially. This is one truth that you can take to the bank.

9. Learn to Work with Other People's Money

Believe it or not, you will probably never grow rich or retire early unless you learn to use other people's money. Look at Donal Trump as a classic example of the success of this principle. He has built up an over five billion dollar personal fortunc by borrowing other people's money and then using it to develop real estate, resorts, casinos, and commercial properties over the decades.

Better still, he brings in banks and other investors as junior partners, and then he does not even have to pay back the money that they put into the ventures from his own. You can do this too, even if it is on a smaller scale.

10. Continue to Improve Your Financial Education

You should never stop learning until the day that you pass away. This is especially true where your financial education is concerned. Every day you should make it a point to read some kind of useful financial publication, whether it is Bloomberg online, the Wall Street Journal, Forbes, Money Magazine, or the Economist.

All of these well respected publications will teach you how to manage your money and invest more effectively. Keep the reading mantra going with books and workshops on finances too.

11. Become an Investor

Hopefully you are among the elite people who consider themselves to be savers. Saving is only the start of the journey towards wealth and retirement, not an ends in itself. You must make the next leap into the more exclusive investor category if you want to get ahead of the pack and truly succeed financially. This is where that last point about building up your financial education is especially important.

Schools still teach us to be employees as their methods of teaching are still based on the industrial age. In order to become an investor you must teach yourself or find a good mentor. The best way to learn is to practice with someone who is already a successful investor.

12. Write And Follow Your Action Plan

All of these twelve principles are noble goals. Noble goals that you do not write down and follow up on will be nothing more than altruistic ideas, also known as wishful thinking. Do not become a victim of the "could have, should have, would have" syndrome.

- Write down your concrete actionable steps and start working down this list today.
- Where do you want to be in 1 year, 2 years , 10 and 20 years from now?
- Where do you see yourself living?
- What will you do?
- How much income will you have?
- Where will your income come from?

These twelve principles are essential cornerstones in any effort to reach true wealth, financial freedom and an early retirement. When you put them into action, then you will begin to see results that start out as small at first but gradually snowball into real measurable progress.

The Elevation Group - Mike Dillard - Wealth Training Review

In the difficult economic times today that are often compared to the Great Recession of the 1930's, there could be a silver lining. You may not have heard that more people became millionaires during the Great Depression than at any other point in history.

This is because when there is great upheaval, tremendous opportunity presents itself. Mike Dillard of the Elevation Group is an individual who believes this so strongly that he offers free wealth training for you when you go to his site. Read on to learn who Mike Dillard is, what the Elevation Group is about, and the kind of training that they offer you at no charge.

Who Is Mike Dillard?

Mike Dillard is a man who has turned his personal fortunes around from being a waiter into a millionaire by the time he reached age twenty-six. This feat alone deserves your attention. During the last five years, he started two publishing firms that enjoyed a total combined twenty million dollars in revenues. He runs an online newsletter that counts more than a million entrepreneurs in sixty-five countries as subscribers. The Elevation Group is his latest endeavor.

What is the Elevation Group?

Mike Dillard formed the Elevation Group because he has an urgent message and training that he wants to offer individuals all over the globe. He realizes that he is not a money manager or investment adviser, so he put together a collection of individuals who are extremely good in their various fields to help him.

Using the combined talents of these people who together make hundreds of millions of dollars from their investments, he offers you access to the techniques and strategies that rich people utilize to protect, invest, and increase their wealth in these difficult economic times that you live.

The purpose behind Mike Dillard starting the Elevation Group was originally to increase his own financial education and yours along the way. In this group, he shares his own experiences of where he is investing his own money and allows you to gain knowledge from his good and bad experiences. The Elevation Group especially targets you who are interested in building up a residual income through a business at home.

The Elevation Group offers a membership website for people who wish to learn the ways to efficiently manage and invest their money. This program is separate from the free seminar training. Some of what his free wealth training encompasses will surprise you, and it is a message to which you should listen carefully.

What is Mike Dillard's Track Record Using The Information in His Training?

During the last few years, Dillard points out that most people have lost anywhere from thirty to forty percent on their investments.

At the same time, he used the information that he offers in his training seminars to incredible effect. He has banked gains of over four hundred and seventy percent in the last thirty six months alone.

What Does This Free Wealth Training Cover?

The main message that Mike Dillard wants to teach you about is that you can become incredibly wealthy in times where there is economic turmoil. This is true whether or not you have much money now to invest. He starts out by telling you that there are two different sets of approaches to investing. The middle class have one, while the wealthy have a completely different set of rules. His training covers the ways that the rich are incredibly growing their wealth in one of the worst economic crisis in history.

He is able to predict what will happen to the U.S. economically during the coming several months to three years. It is not a pretty picture that he is describing. Mike claims that ninety-five percent of the population will be bankrupted by it, and that this has happened in thirty nations over the last hundred years. His message of hope is that you can protect and exponentially increase your wealth if you know what to do.

Mike Dillard teaches you three main nuggets in this five part training. You will learn how you can grow fantastically wealthy in any time where there is economic turbulence and chaos. You will come to understand the ways that you can create a hundred thousand dollar each month retirement strategy which is completely tax free. You will also learn what will happen to the American economy in the future six months to thirty-six months and what you can do to make incredible profits in these months.

Mike offers this training in the form of a free seminar that you can select on a given date and time. There are four different dates and times offered. He has a limited two hundred and fifty slots open at every seminar, so you are asked to really tune in and to be on time for the one that you sign up to attend. Besides the seminar where you will be taught these three things, he offers you a bonus video on how you can predict the financial future yourself.

What is the Predict the Financial Future Training About?

Mike Dillard's bonus training video is all about how you are able to predict the financial future. This is a very interesting piece that will teach you a historical perspective in seven steps on what inevitably happens to all great economies and empires over time.

Mike shows you how this seven step process occurs every time and is unavoidable. This is what makes it such a foolproof guide for you. This same guide is the one that the super rich use to forecast the most critical events for the financial future. The rich have already begun to use information to make themselves even wealthier, and you can too.

This video can be described in the following sequence. All great powers go through these seven steps in their economic evolution. They start out with good money that is backed up by gold and/or silver. They then pile on social programs that increase the country's financial burdens.

They next increase their military spending as their economic influence grows. These lead to wars as a result of a powerful military. The country or empire then leaves its sound precious metal backed money for a Fiat currency that only has value because the government says it does, like the U.S. did in 1971.

Inflation then rolls in, as you have seen in commodities prices rising by more than forty-six percent over the last few years. Finally, a wealth transfer happens as the smart people leave the collapsing currency in favor of precious metals.

Mike teaches you that we are in between the inflation stage and the wealth transfer stage now. You who have the foresight to protect yourself against this will gain from an enormous transfer of wealth as the currency collapses. He calls this the largest transfer of wealth in history. If you do not do anything about it, then you will be ruined by inflation and the fall of the U.S. dollar and other fiat currencies. He knows this because all past fiat currencies have always failed.

Should you not go learn from his free training about how to protect and grow your wealth before today's inflation turns into tomorrow's fiat currency crisis?

<u>RESOURCES</u>

"Free Bonus Content"

Resources

For additional 'Wealth Advisor' editions please check our website or go to amazon.com.

Get All 'Wealth Advisor' Editions
www.wealthbuildingcourse.com/wealth-advisor

At present we are offering a free membership to the Wealth Building Course. This membership is free as long the full course is in development. The current release date will we in 2012 and the course will be priced at $799.

Sign Up For Your Free Wealth Education Membership:
www.wealthbuildingcourse.com

If you have additional interest in preserving your wealth and invest in silver please check out the author's book: 'Building Wealth with Silver', which is available at amazon.

Building Wealth with Silver Book:
www.wealthbuildingcourse.com/silver-book

The author also developed a very sophisticated course around silver investment, which is available for purchase online. The 'Silver Fortune Formula' course reveals every detail for successful silver investing.

Silver Investment 101:
www.wealthbuildingcourse.com/silver

Thomas Herold, CEO – Co-founder Wealth Building Course

Thomas Hcrold is a successful entrepreneur and personal development coach. After a career with one of the largest electronic companies in the world, he realized that a regular job would never fully satisfy his need for connection on a deep level.

The only way to live his full potential was to start building his own business and find new ways to be in service to others.

For over 25 years he has helped many people – including himself – build their dream businesses. Toward that goal, he focuses on education – simplified and enhanced by modern technology. He is the author of three books with over 200,000 copies distributed worldwide.

Other than his passion for creating businesses, Thomas has spent over 20 years in the self-development field. Placing emphasis on the exploration of consciousness and building practical applications that allow people to express their purpose and passion in life, Thomas's work in this area has provided ample and happy proof that this approach works.

He believes that every person has at least one gift and that, when this gift is developed and nourished, it will serve as a fountainhead of personal happiness and help contribute to a better, more sustainable world.

For the past three years Thomas Herold has studied the monetary system and has experienced some profound insights on how money and wealth are related. He has recently committed to sharing this knowledge in a new venture – the Wealth Building Course, a website along with educational materials that designed to help people get started on their own money makeover and get a financial education in the process.

Thomas's ultimate vision for the Wealth Building Course is to empower people to adopt a wealthy mindset and to create abundance for themselves and others. His ability to explain complex information in simple terms makes him an outstanding teacher and coach.